# DINOWORLD

# REALM OF THE DINOSAURS

# DINOWORLD

# REALM OF THE
# DINOSAURS

KINGFISHER
Larousse Kingfisher Chambers Inc.
95 Madison Avenue
New York, New York 10016

First published in 1998
10 9 8 7 6 5 4 3 2 1

Copyright © Larousse plc 1998

LIBRARY OF CONGRESS CATALOGING-IN-PUBLICATION DATA
Realm of the dinosaurs / Michael
Benton..[et al.] 1st American ed.
        p. cm.—(Dinoworld)
    Includes index.
    Summary: Presents facts about dinosaurs
including their physical characteristics,
habitat, enemies, diet, behavior, why they
disappeared, how they were rediscovered,
and some of their present-day descendents.

1. Dinosaurs—Juvenile literature.
[1. Dinosaurs.]   I. Benton, Michael, 1939-
II. Series.
QE862.D5R354  1998  567.9—dc21
97—32765
CIP AC
ISBN: 0-7534-5159-X

Written by: Michael Benton, Dougal Dixon,
   Glenn W. Storrs, and David Unwin
Edited by: Michéle Byam, Jackie Gaff, Claire
   Llewellyn, Jenny Siklós
Designed by: Shaun Barlow, Primrose
   Burton, David West Children's Book
   Design, Smiljka Surla, Terry Woodley
Dinoventures written by: Jim Miles
Illustrated by: Robby Braun, Chris Forsey,
   Steve Kirk, Bernard Long, Temple Rogers,
   Doreen McGuiness, Myke Taylor

Printed in Italy

# Contents

# The World of Brachiosaurus

## Period: Late Jurassic— 150 million years ago

Who can imagine standing next to *Brachiosaurus*, its head appearing to disappear into the clouds! Well, perhaps not the clouds, but at 13 feet (4m) above the ground, I'd rather watch *Brachiosaurus* out of a third-floor window. This kind of dinosaur, one of more than one hundred species of sauropods (meaning "reptile feet"), would have taken your breath away, no matter which way you looked at them.

*Brachiosaurus* was some 80 feet (25m) long and weighed at least 50 tons, about as heavy as ten elephants. And there were sauropods who were longer and heavier still. At present, the record appears to be an animal named *Seismosaurus* ("Earth-shaking reptile"), which reached almost 130 feet (40m) in length and may have weighed as much as 75 tons.

Such sizable land-living creatures would have had an enormous appetite. Just how much would it take to feed a *Brachiosaurus*? For such a large animal, the mouth is rather small and there are no chewing teeth to chomp up the leaves and branches before they are swallowed. Stomach stones helped remedy this funny situation, but even so, these sauropods must have spent all day, and most of the night, feeding on the leaves of tall trees, much as giraffes do today. It must have taken huge amounts of vegetation to keep a sauropod's stomach from rumbling. But what's this about tall trees? Didn't *Brachiosaurus* and its relatives live in lakes and swamps? Didn't they need to support their heavy bulk by buoying themselves up in deep water? In a word: "No." We now know that animals like *Brachiosaurus* were no more stuck in the water than are animals like rhinoceroses today. These giant dinosaurs were thorough-going land animals. You are going to read about some of the most spectacular creatures ever to have lived on land. With their small heads, long tails, and enormous bodies, they are like fantasy animals, too big to have really existed—only they did exist! Turn the page to begin the sauropod adventure.

**David B. Weishampel**
*Associate Professor*
Johns Hopkins University

# BRACHIOSAURUS TIMELINE

One of the best known periods in the history of the dinosaurs is the late Jurassic. Dinosaurs had already been around for over 60 million years, and they now completely dominated life on land. The sauropods, such as *Brachiosaurus*, *Dicraeosaurus*, and *Camarasaurus*, were at the height of their reign as the main plant-eating dinosaurs. They lived alongside other herbivores, such as *Dryosaurus* and *Camptosaurus*, whose descendants, the iguanodontids and hadrosaurids, would largely replace the sauropods in the Cretaceous period.

6 *Dicraeosaurus*

2 *Camptosaurus*

5 *Dryosaurus*

▶ The "Age of Reptiles," or Mesozoic era, lasted from approximately 245 million to 65 million years ago. The Jurassic period was the middle portion of the dinosaur "age," coming after the Triassic and before the Cretaceous. The largest known dinosaurs lived during the late Jurassic.

4 *Elaphrosaurus*

LATE   TRIASSIC                                        JURASSIC

| | | Early | Middle | |
|---|---|---|---|---|

Millions of Years Ago

230        220        210        200        190        180        170        160

▼ The late Jurassic earth shook as herds of *Dicraeosaurus* and *Brachiosaurus* tramped along in search of plant fodder. These moving mountains of flesh were trailed by meat-eating ceratosaurs, hoping to pick off the young or the weak. Many herbivores developed defensive techniques. While sauropods relied on sheer size, *Stegosaurus* armed itself with long spikes, and *Dryosaurus* evolved long, powerful, high-speed legs.

1 *Brachiosaurus*

3 *Ceratosaurus*

CRETACEOUS

Early

Late

145   130   110   100  95  90   80   70  65

# 150 MILLION YEARS AGO

The face of the Earth is continually changing as the continents slowly drift apart to form new oceans, or collide with each other to produce mountain chains. Early in the Dinosaur Age, the continents were massed together in a single supercontinent called Pangaea. By the late Jurassic, Pangaea had broken up into Laurasia in the north, and Gondwanaland in the south.

▼ In the late Jurassic, rising sea levels had drowned much of Europe and separated Asia from the other continents. However, Africa and North America, were joined part of the time, and many of the same dinosaurs were found on both continents.

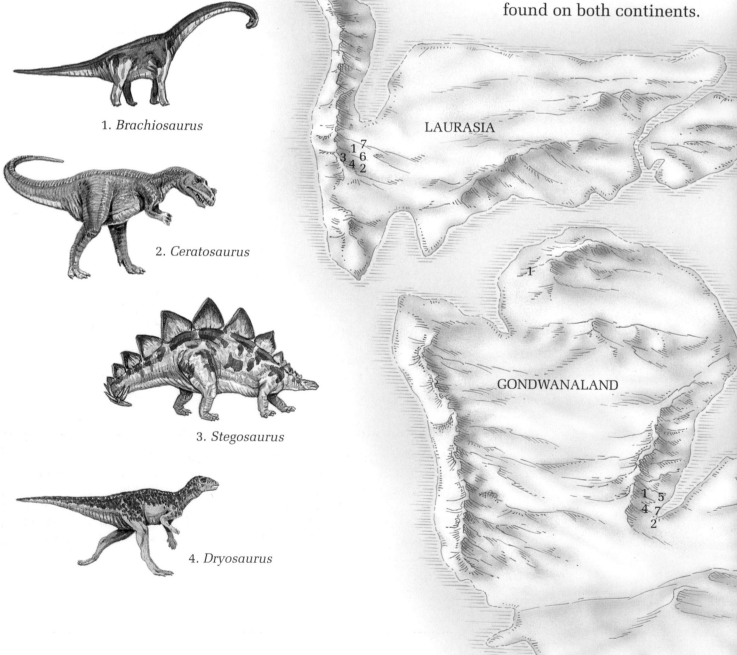

1. *Brachiosaurus*

2. *Ceratosaurus*

3. *Stegosaurus*

4. *Dryosaurus*

LAURASIA

GONDWANALAND

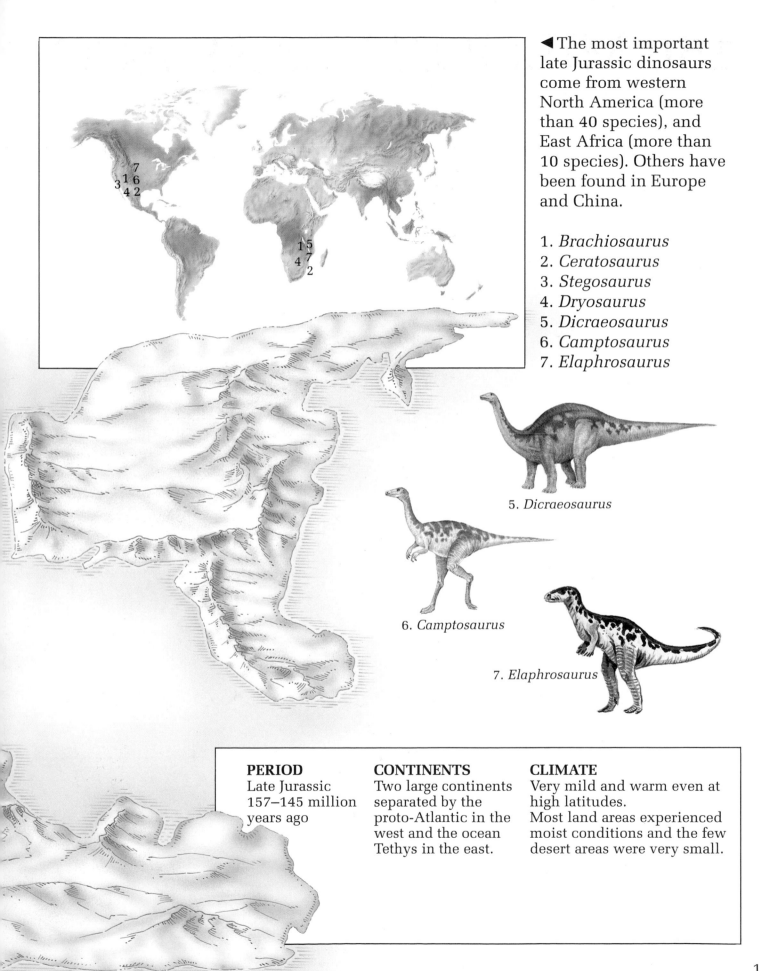

◄ The most important late Jurassic dinosaurs come from western North America (more than 40 species), and East Africa (more than 10 species). Others have been found in Europe and China.

1. *Brachiosaurus*
2. *Ceratosaurus*
3. *Stegosaurus*
4. *Dryosaurus*
5. *Dicraeosaurus*
6. *Camptosaurus*
7. *Elaphrosaurus*

5. *Dicraeosaurus*

6. *Camptosaurus*

7. *Elaphrosaurus*

**PERIOD**
Late Jurassic 157–145 million years ago

**CONTINENTS**
Two large continents separated by the proto-Atlantic in the west and the ocean Tethys in the east.

**CLIMATE**
Very mild and warm even at high latitudes.
Most land areas experienced moist conditions and the few desert areas were very small.

# PREHISTORIC TENDAGURU

*Brachiosaurus* lived in an area that paleontologists call Tendaguru, in what is now East Africa, on a flat coastal plain covered with conifer forests and areas of more open vegetation. Shallow rivers flowed across the plain, feeding through marshy deltas into a shallow sea, which lay to the east. Occasionally this sea flooded the area, forcing the dinosaurs to move elsewhere for food.

▼ A herd of *Brachiosaurus* use their long necks to harvest the upper branches of Tendaguru conifers.

▼ A large, primitive lacewing unfolds its paired wings before it lifts off into the Jurassic sky.

► *Kentrosaurus* was a tanklike, plant-eating dinosaur, that had plates and spines for armor. Here, it is plodding along in search of low-growing vegetation to eat. Its plates and spines protected it from small predators.

▲ Conifers and ferns provided most of the ground cover, mixed with cycads and ginkgoes.

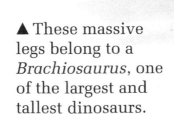

▲ These massive legs belong to a *Brachiosaurus*, one of the largest and tallest dinosaurs.

▲ Small pterosaurs hunt for insects, stirred up by *Brachiosaurus* as it lumbers through the undergrowth.

▲ *Dryosaurus*, a fast-moving herbivore, keeps a lookout for predators.

# THE TENDAGURU COMMUNITIES

In Tendaguru, two different communities lived side by side; one on the land and one in the sea. Dinosaurs dominated the land community. Plants supported the many herbivorous dinosaurs, which were eaten by carnivorous dinosaurs. Plants also provided food and shelter for insects, the main diet of lizards and pterosaurs. Out in the shallow, warm sea, small fish were preyed upon by sharks, marine reptiles, and fish-eating pterosaurs.

### Pterosaurs

Skimming over the surface of the sea, the pterosaur *Rhamphorhynchus* used its long, sharp, pointed beak to scoop up fish.

### Sharks

Early sharks such as *Hybodus* were common in Jurassic seas, polishing off the dead, the dying, and the unwary.

## Insects

Most Jurassic insects fed on plants. Some insects tackled larger animals, living as parasites on dinosaur skin or by sucking dinosaur blood.

Cockroach

Mayfly

Water boatman

Water scorpion

Dragonfly

## Pterosaurs

With powerful beats of its long wings, *Anurognathus* pursued insects, such as lacewings, engulfing them in its wide open jaws.

## Lizards

Sphenodontids were small lizardlike reptiles that fed on plants or insects. A single species, the Tuatara, still lives in parts of New Zealand.

## Sea reptiles

*Pleurosaurus*, and many other reptiles, took to a life in the seas, evolving long streamlined bodies, and flipperlike fore and hind limbs.

## Fish

Many fish lived in the coral reefs off the Tendaguru coast. *Gyrodus* broke open coral with rows of crushing teeth, in order to feed on polyps.

15

# ENEMIES AND COMPETITORS

Careful studies of their fossil remains show that, like modern animals, each of the Tendaguru dincsaurs lived in its own particular way. *Brachiosaurus* and the other sauropods played the role of heavyweight herbivores, like elephants and buffaloes. *Kentrosaurus* looks like a Jurassic rhinoceros, while, at a distance, herds of *Dryosaurus* might easily be mistaken for kangaroos. Their enemies were predators such as *Ceratosaurus*, much larger and more dangerous than modern lions, and the small high-speed killer, *Elaphrosaurus*, which may have hunted in packs as jackals do today. Instead of birds, the air was filled with pterosaurs.

▶ Adult brachiosaurs were too large to deal with. But, if a young animal became separated from the herd, *Ceratosaurus* pounced, killing its victim with a few swift bites. A few tons of fresh brachiosaur lasted for days!

**Kentrosaurus**

KEN-tro-SAW-rus
"SPIKY REPTILE"
17 FT. (5 M) LONG

*Kentrosaurus* was a stegosaur, with plates and sharp, pointed spines running down its back.

### Ceratosaurus

SER-a-toe-SAW-rus
"HORNED REPTILE"
20 FT. (6 M) LONG

Only great size or great speed could save you from this Jurassic terminator that was armed with bladelike teeth.

# DOWN IN THE UNDERGROWTH

Not all dinosaurs were giants. *Dryosaurus* was a small, lightly built animal. The short forelimbs and five-fingered hands were used to scratch up roots or tear up vegetation. Using a long stiffened tail to balance on its powerful hind limbs, this was a fast and agile dinosaur, capable of outrunning anything, except perhaps *Elaphrosaurus*. Dryosaurs were also very efficient feeders, nipping off leaves or fronds with their bony beaks, storing them in cheek pouches, and then chopping them up with sharp, chisellike teeth.

**Dryosaurus**

DRY-o-SAW-rus
"OAK REPTILE"
13 FT. (4 M) LONG

The herd of *Dryosaurus* are keeping a wary eye on the *Elaphrosaurus* pack, now feasting on their sibling.

**Elaphrosaurus**

ee-LAF-roe-
SAW-rus
"LIGHTWEIGHT
REPTILE"
11.6 FT. (3.5 M)
LONG

A fast-moving and
dangerous predator,
which probably
hunted in packs.

# THE TALLEST DINOSAUR?

Capable of peering over a three-story house,
*Brachiosaurus* was one of the tallest animals ever
found. In some ways it was like other sauropod
dinosaurs: a giant size, with a small head, a long
neck, and a long tail. The limbs were stout and
pillarlike, in order to support the enormous body
weight—though some of the load was reduced by
hollow, air-filled spaces in the neck bones.
Unlike most sauropods, where the neck was
held level, *Brachiosaurus* could lift its neck
up almost upright. As the forelimbs were
much longer than the hind limbs, this gave
*Brachiosaurus* an enormous reach, like that of the
giraffe, only much higher.

## COMPARING FEET

*Brachiosaurus*'s front feet
had to bear a lot of
weight. So, like modern
elephants' feet, the toes
were very short and
clustered together.

African elephant

Claw

▶ In order to achieve a high enough pressure to pump the blood all the way up to the brain, *Brachiosaurus* had a huge heart. It weighed over one ton.

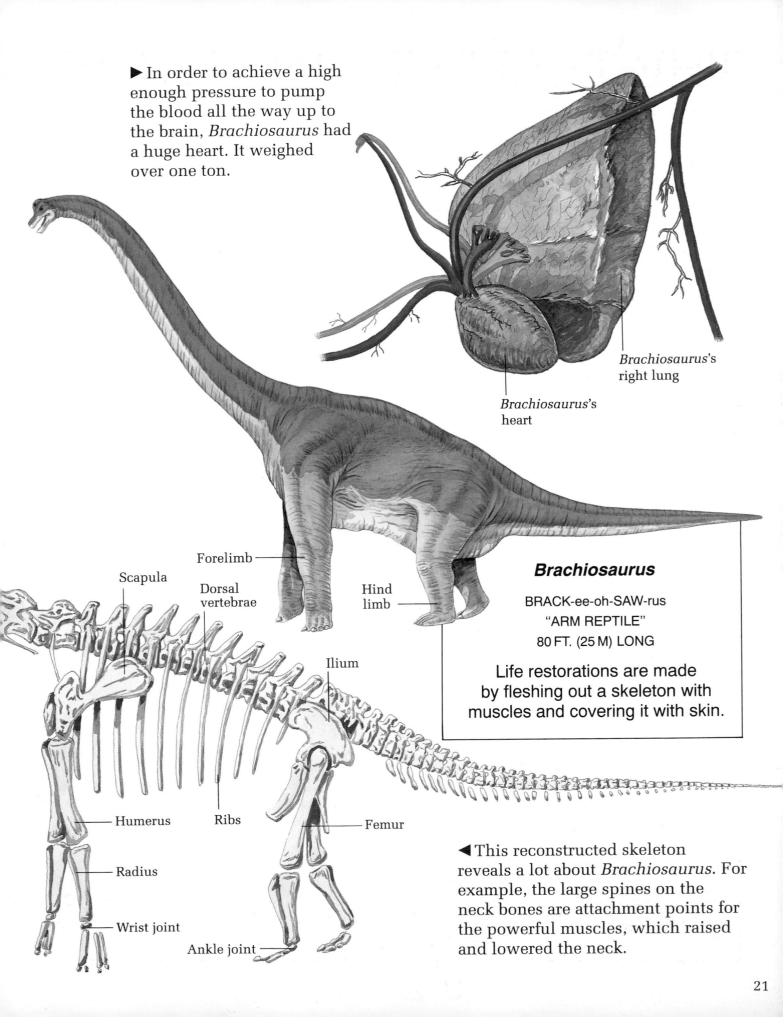

*Brachiosaurus*'s right lung

*Brachiosaurus*'s heart

Forelimb

Scapula

Dorsal vertebrae

Hind limb

Ilium

**_Brachiosaurus_**

BRACK-ee-oh-SAW-rus
"ARM REPTILE"
80 FT. (25 M) LONG

Life restorations are made by fleshing out a skeleton with muscles and covering it with skin.

Humerus

Ribs

Femur

Radius

Wrist joint

Ankle joint

◀ This reconstructed skeleton reveals a lot about *Brachiosaurus*. For example, the large spines on the neck bones are attachment points for the powerful muscles, which raised and lowered the neck.

# THE INCREDIBLE EATING MACHINE

All large herbivores have a problem in common—in order to avoid starvation they have to eat almost continuously. It was even worse for *Brachiosaurus*—not only was it a gigantic size, but all its food had to pass through a very small head. How did it solve this difficult problem? Perhaps *Brachiosaurus* had a slower lifestyle than other living herbivores and so didn't need to eat so much. Even so, it must have eaten between 100 and 400 pounds (50 and 200 kg) of plants a day. Feeding almost constantly, *Brachiosaurus* used chisellike teeth to rake vegetation into its mouth. Its food was digested as it passed through the intestines. The waste reemerged at the other end as large droppings.

▶ *Brachiosaurus*'s huge body was almost entirely filled with guts. These were yards of intestine, and an enormous stomach that gurgled away with stewed vegetation.

Vertebrae

Lung

Heart

Gizzard

Large intestine

## STOMACH STONES

Conifer leaves made up the bulk of *Brachiosaurus*'s diet, supplemented by cycads and ginkgoes. As some heavily worn teeth show, this was tough stuff. *Brachiosaurus* didn't chew its food, but ground it up in its gizzard, using specially swallowed stones (gastroliths).

Gastroliths

Plant food

▼ Herds of *Brachiosaurus* and *Barosaurus*, eating almost continuously, had a devastating effect on the local vegetation. The other Tendaguru herbivores fed among the undergrowth, eating those plants which the sauropods left behind. So, each animal had its own way of life and avoided direct competition with its neighbors.

## HIGH

*Brachiosaurus* was a high browser, reaching up with its long neck to feed on the tops of trees.

## MIDDLE

*Barosaurus* was a middle-level browser, feeding on bushes and the lower branches of conifers.

## LOW

*Kentrosaurus* and *Dryosaurus* were low-level browsers, grazing on small plants such as ferns.

# GENTLE GIANTS OF THE JURASSIC

Paleontologists have long puzzled over a most important question—what was *Brachiosaurus*'s way of life? Living animals don't help because there is nothing like *Brachiosaurus* on Earth today. Fortunately, fossils provide us with clues as to how extinct animals lived. Details of the teeth show what kinds of foods were eaten. The shape of the skull and the size of the eyes and nostrils, show how important the senses were. How animals walked is revealed by the size and shape of the limb bones. This kind of evidence gives us an accurate picture of how dinosaurs lived.

▼ Perhaps *Brachiosaurus* supported its great weight by living under water, using the nostrils on top of its skull to "snorkel," and eating water plants with its simple teeth. But this can't be right, because the water pressure would have stopped *Brachiosaurus* from breathing.

◄ Perhaps *Brachiosaurus* galloped around and reared up on its hind limbs. In fact, it was too heavy to run, and wouldn't have stood on two legs in case it fell and injured itself.

► A slow lifestyle seems most likely. Fossil trackways show that *Brachiosaurus* ambled around at a gentle pace and, most surprisingly, probably lived in family groups.

# A DINOSAUR GRAVEYARD

The fates of Tendaguru dinosaurs were many and varied. Most never became fossils because they were eaten by scavengers or decayed away. As carcasses floated down rivers and out to sea, odd bones, parts of the spine, even whole limbs, sometimes dropped away and became buried in sediment. Great concentrations of skeletons, all belonging to *Kentrosaurus* or *Dryosaurus*, have been found piled together. After the droughts that caused these mass deaths, the carcasses were heaped together by floods during the rainy season.

▼ Occasionally the big sauropods became trapped in boggy areas. The exposed parts of the body decayed away, or were carried off by scavengers, attracted by the smell of rotting flesh.

## SCAVENGERS

Light enough to cross the mud without getting stuck, *Elaphrosaurus* prepares to feast on the huge carcasses of dead and dying brachiosaurs.

▼ Herbivore bones with bite marks, and broken carnivore teeth, show that meat-eating dinosaurs scavenged sauropod carcasses. Other scavengers included late Jurassic crocodiles.

# BRACHIOSAURUS'S RELATIVES

Sauropods survived to the end of the Dinosaur Age. But they were far less numerous in the Cretaceous period, making way for plant-eating ornithopod dinosaurs, like *Iguanodon*. *Brachiosaurus*'s own line survived into the early Cretaceous, where it is represented by an English dinosaur, *Pelorosaurus*. The most important late Cretaceous sauropods were the titanosaurs, which include some remarkable dinosaurs: *Hypselosaurus*, one of the few sauropods for which fossil eggs are known; a miniature sauropod, *Magyarosaurus*; and two armored sauropods from South America, *Titanosaurus* and *Saltasaurus*.

## *Saltasaurus*

SALT-a-SAW-rus
"SALTA REPTILE"
40 FT. (12 M) LONG

## BODY ARMOR

*Saltasaurus*'s back and upper sides were protected by armor, consisting of large, oval bony plates, surrounded by small bony studs.

## *Abelisaurus*

ah-BELL-i-SAW-rus
"ABEL'S REPTILE"

A recently discovered large theropod; its length is unknown.

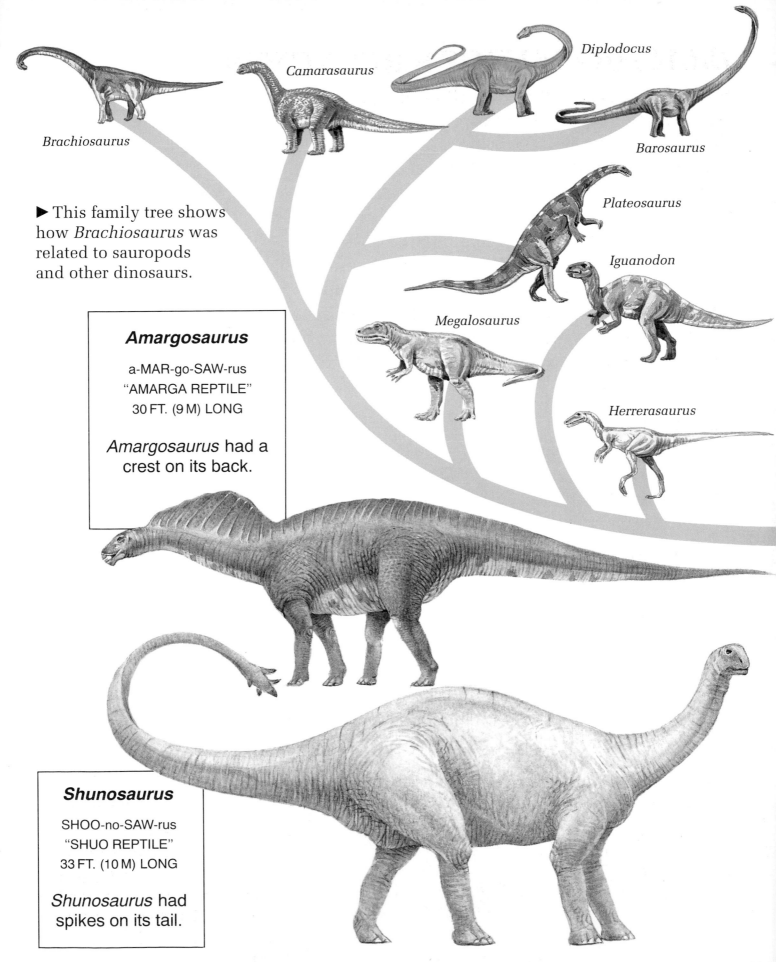

Brachiosaurus

Camarasaurus

Diplodocus

Barosaurus

Plateosaurus

Iguanodon

Megalosaurus

Herrerasaurus

▶ This family tree shows how *Brachiosaurus* was related to sauropods and other dinosaurs.

**Amargosaurus**

a-MAR-go-SAW-rus
"AMARGA REPTILE"
30 FT. (9 M) LONG

*Amargosaurus* had a crest on its back.

**Shunosaurus**

SHOO-no-SAW-rus
"SHUO REPTILE"
33 FT. (10 M) LONG

*Shunosaurus* had spikes on its tail.

# DINOSAUR GIANTS

Dinosaurs outperformed living animals in a number of ways, most especially in their size. *Brachiosaurus* may have weighed up to ten times more than the largest land animal, the African elephant (6 tons). However, some dinosaurs may have been twice the size of *Brachiosaurus*! How do we calculate the size of a dinosaur? With a complete dinosaur, such as *Brachiosaurus*, the height and length can be measured directly from the skeleton. Rough estimates of a dinosaur's weight can be found by measuring a model.

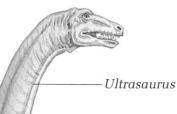

— *Ultrasaurus*

▼ Many groups of animals have taken advantage of being large. It is more energy efficient, and bigger animals are better able to compete for food and mates. Large size also helps to frighten off predators.

## *Ultrasaurus*

ULL-tra-SAW-rus
"ULTRA REPTILE"
97 FT. (30 M) LONG

This brachiosaurid from the late Jurassic of Colorado, may have weighed over 150 tons.

## Seismosaurus

SIZE-mo-SAW-rus
"EARTH-SHAKING REPTILE"
130 FT. (40 M) LONG

A diplodocid from the late
Jurassic of the United States. Only
the spine and hips have been found.

## Supersaurus

SUPER-SAW-rus
"SUPER REPTILE"
80–100 FT. (25–30 M) LONG

A diplodocid from the
late Jurassic of
Colorado. It may
have weighed less
than *Brachiosaurus*.

▼ There is a maximum likely size for animals (between 100–200 tons), and it looks like sauropods reached it. However, such large size brings lots of problems. Just to keep going, these dinosaurs had to eat almost continuously. Also, because of their relatively small surface area, there was a severe risk of heat stroke. Perhaps their long necks helped to get rid of excess heat.

*Supersaurus*

*Brachiosaurus*

◄ *Brachiosaurus* had a length of about 80 feet (25 m) and a head height of 40 feet (12 m). It probably weighed at least 50 tons, although estimates of its weight vary from as little as 15, to as much as 78 tons.

# DINOFACTS

**Q**: What sort of skin did *Brachiosaurus* have, and what color was it?

An African elephant

**A**: Skin is not preserved in any *Brachiosaurus*. But judging by living reptiles and other dinosaurs where skin has been found, it was probably very thick, tough. and scaly. In color, *Brachiosaurus* was probably just a fairly drab green or brown; like elephants, they were just too big to mess with, so they didn't need camouflage coloration.

**Q**: Could *Brachiosaurus* make any sounds?

**A**: Like living reptiles, *Brachiosaurus* could probably only hiss or grunt, but it might also have been able to honk or hoot by forcing air out through its partly closed nostrils.

**Q**: Did *Brachiosaurus* lay eggs like other dinosaurs?

**A**: *Brachiosaurus* eggs have never been found, but descendants of *Brachiosaurus* appear to have laid large eggs over 10 inches (25 cm) in diameter and with rough pebbly areas. When the baby hatched it weighed about 20 pounds (10 kg) and measured about 3 feet (1 m) long.

**Q**: How intelligent was *Brachiosaurus*?

**A**: Weight for weight *Brachiosaurus* has the smallest brain of almost any dinosaur, only one-hundred-thousandth of its body weight (the human brain is one-fortieth of human body weight). Evidently this huge, plant-eating plodder was no Jurassic mastermind.

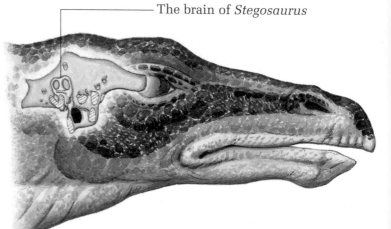

The brain of *Stegosaurus*

A fossilized egg of the sauropod *Hypselosaurus* compared to a chicken's egg.

**Q**: Did *Brachiosaurus* live in herds?

**A**: Probably yes. Many trackways that seem to have been made by groups of slow-moving animals are now known. Sometimes the skeletons of many animals are found preserved together. These *Brachiosaurus* graveyards are possibly the remains of a herd that ran (or rather plodded) into some kind of natural disaster.

A giant tortoise

**Q**: How long did a *Brachiosaurus* live?

**A**: It is well known that, in general, large animals live longer than small ones; elephants reach up to 70 years of age, for example, and some large reptiles such as tortoises are known to have existed for over 150 years. *Brachiosaurus*, a gigantic reptile, probably lived for over a hundred years, and possibly much longer.

▲ Trackways of a sauropod and a theropod dinosaur

▼ Hadrosaurs, such as *Parasaurolophus* from North America, may have competed with Cretaceous sauropods for food.

**Q**: Why is *Brachiosaurus* not alive today?

**A**: Animal species don't last that long; a few million years at most. *Brachiosaurus* probably only lasted a few million years, but its descendants carried on the line for at least another 40 million years. Eventually they too died out, perhaps because of changes in the climate or the vegetation, or perhaps from competition with other more efficient plant-eating dinosaurs such as hadrosaurs.

# FINDING *BRACHIOSAURUS*

As the 20th century dawned, one of the great paleontological discoveries of all time was made at Tendaguru, in Tanzania, East Africa. Between 1908 and 1912, an expedition, led by Janensch and Hennig from the Humboldt Museum in Berlin, discovered thousands of dinosaur bones, including those of *Brachiosaurus*. Conditions were very difficult. It was stiflingly hot and there was a serious risk of catching malaria. Despite this, the expedition was very successful and over 250 tons of bones were collected by teams of up to 500 excavators.

▼ Bones were encased in plaster and wrapped in grass and bamboo. Then they had to be carried 60 miles (96 kms) to the coast, to be shipped to Germany.

► Standing over 40 feet (12 m) high, the fully mounted specimen of *Brachiosaurus* in the Humboldt Museum, Berlin, is one of the world's largest and most spectacular dinosaur exhibits.

▲ Over 80 articulated skeletons and thousands of isolated bones were collected. The largest bones measured nearly 10 feet (3 m) long, and weighed as much as 550 pounds (250 kg).

# The World of Stegosaurus

## *Period: Late Jurassic—150 million years ago*

Stegosaurus—that dinosaur with the plates on its back and spikes on its tail—is one of those classic dinosaurs of yesteryear. It was originally discovered over a century ago, when the states of Colorado and Wyoming, where it was found, had not had their boundaries drawn, when the Native Americans ruled the Plains, and when dinosaur paleontology was just in its infancy. It was animals like this strange plated and spiked dinosaur that gave people their first glimpse of the richness of dinosaurs in North America.

Over the years, paleontologists have speculated about the lifestyle of *Stegosaurus.* They have focused not only on how the plates and spikes were used, but also why this dinosaur appeared to have such a small brain. Were the plates used for protection against *Allosaurus* and *Ceratosaurus,* meat-eating neighbors of *Stegosaurus*? Were the plates movable? Did they come in a double or a single row? Were they for display? Or did they function as air conditioners and solar panels?

And what of the spikes at the end of the tail? Surely they could have inflicted severe gouges in the legs and even face of a meat-eater who came too close! But all of this seems a bit too clever for an animal with very little brain power. For *Stegosaurus*—as well as other kinds of plated and spiked dinosaurs—had very small brains, so small in fact that paleontologists looked elsewhere for centers of stegosaur thought, such as between the hips. An intellectual center here seems unlikely, but even so there was space for one! All of these questions and other oddities have surrounded *Stegosaurus* since we began learning about it. The story of *Stegosaurus* and its relatives is a very important one in our understanding of dinosaurs. As part of the early discoveries in North America, *Stegosaurus* gave us our first taste of some of the unusual shapes and sizes of dinosaurs. The life and world of this plated dinosaur continues to fascinate us even today.

**David B. Weishampel**
*Associate Professor*
Johns Hopkins University

# STEGOSAURUS TIMELINE

The late Jurassic is known for its many plant-eating dinosaur species. Both *Brachiosaurus* and *Stegosaurus* were among these gentle giants. Large sauropods like *Apatosaurus* and *Camarasaurus* were dominant, but smaller animals like *Camptosaurus* and *Dryosaurus* were also common. All of these animals were threatened by the hunter *Allosaurus*, which killed and ate other dinosaurs for food. *Stegosaurus* and others evolved bony defenses against *Allosaurus* and its relations. The defenses grew more elaborate, and the attackers grew bigger, up until the end of the "Age of Dinosaurs."

*Camarasaurus*

*Ceratosaurus*

▶ The Jurassic period lasted from about 205 million to 145 million years ago. Many different kinds of dinosaur appeared during the Jurassic. This included the feathered dinosaurs, which eventually gave rise to modern birds.

*Allosaurus*

*Stegosaurus*

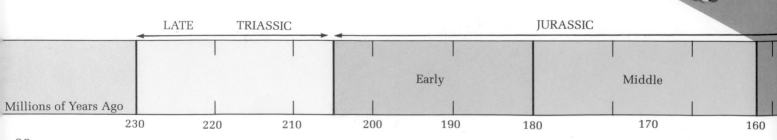

| | LATE | TRIASSIC | | JURASSIC | | |
|---|---|---|---|---|---|---|
| | | | | Early | | Middle |
| Millions of Years Ago | | | | | | |
| 230 | 220 | 210 | 200 | 190 | 180 | 170 | 160 |

— Apatosaurus

▼ Well-known late Jurassic dinosaurs include *Apatosaurus* and *Camarasaurus*. These two giants were plant eaters, as were the smaller *Camptosaurus* and *Dryosaurus*. The meat-eating dinosaurs *Allosaurus* and *Ceratosaurus* preyed on the plant eaters. Different species of early crocodiles and flying pterosaurs shared the dinosaurs' world.

*Camptosaurus*

*Dryosaurus*

CRETACEOUS

| e | Early | Late |
|---|---|---|
| 145 | 130 | 95 90 80 70 65 |

# THE LATE JURASSIC

The Jurassic world was quite different from today's world. The positions of the continents were different and the Atlantic Ocean was just beginning to open. Vast areas of land were low and flat, home to great winding rivers. Lakes and swamps formed from the heavy rains. Mountains were lower than today. North America was partly covered by a warm, shallow sea.

▼ The climate was warmer — monsoonal rain followed long droughts. Lush forests gave plant eaters plenty of food when the rains came. They probably migrated to greener lands in dry times.

1. *Apatosaurus*

2. *Camptosaurus*

3. *Ceratosaurus*

4. *Camarasaurus*

LAURASIA

3
6 5
4
1 2
7

GONDWANALAND

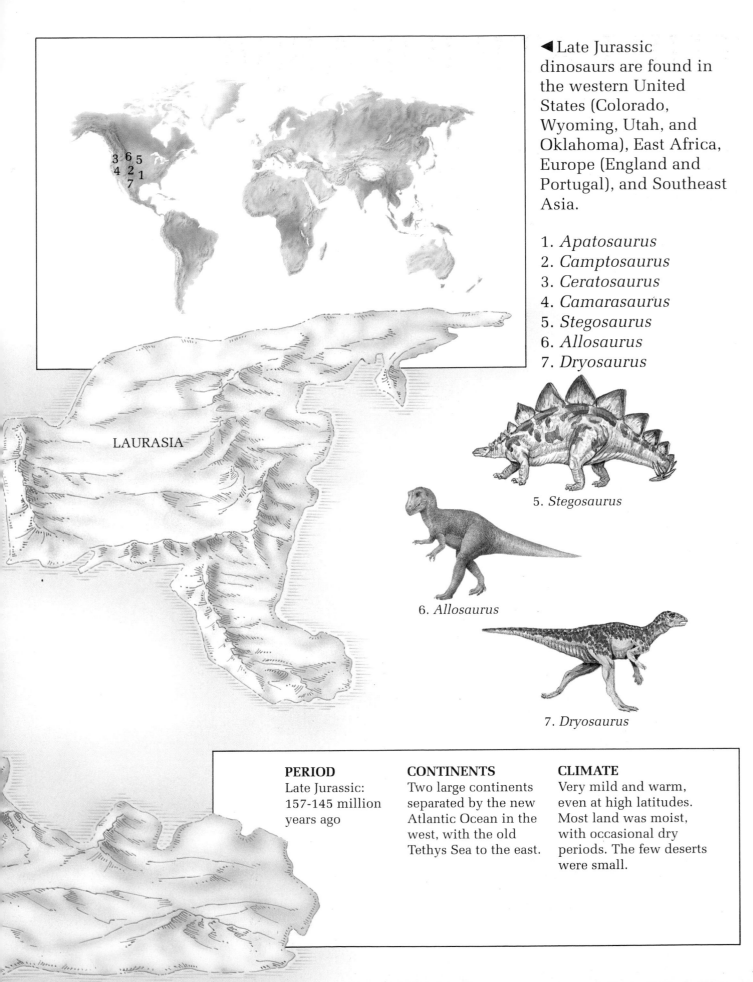

◀ Late Jurassic dinosaurs are found in the western United States (Colorado, Wyoming, Utah, and Oklahoma), East Africa, Europe (England and Portugal), and Southeast Asia.

1. *Apatosaurus*
2. *Camptosaurus*
3. *Ceratosaurus*
4. *Camarasaurus*
5. *Stegosaurus*
6. *Allosaurus*
7. *Dryosaurus*

LAURASIA

5. *Stegosaurus*

6. *Allosaurus*

7. *Dryosaurus*

| **PERIOD** | **CONTINENTS** | **CLIMATE** |
|---|---|---|
| Late Jurassic: 157-145 million years ago | Two large continents separated by the new Atlantic Ocean in the west, with the old Tethys Sea to the east. | Very mild and warm, even at high latitudes. Most land was moist, with occasional dry periods. The few deserts were small. |

# JURASSIC PLAIN

*Stegosaurus* is found in the high plains and Rocky Mountains of North America, in rocks of the Morrison Formation. They were deposited as sediments (sand, mud, and gravel), in huge, slow-moving rivers that once flowed to a warm, shallow sea. The rivers dumped sediments along the way and built great deltas out into the ocean.

▼ Sauropods like *Apatosaurus* walked the flood plains, ate the leaves of tall conifers, and drank from the rivers.

Conifers

▼ *Stegosaurus* lived along the flood plains. Its bones are found in the muds of the long vanished Morrison rivers.

Ferns

▲ Birds like *Archaeopteryx* had feathers, but also teeth and a long tail, like their dinosaur ancestors.

◄ *Allosaurus* was a fearsome predator of the late Jurassic. Wherever plant eaters were found, a hungry *Allosaurus* was probably nearby.

Horsetails ——

◄ *Diplosaurus* lived in the rivers and lakes. Modern crocodiles have changed little from this ancient form.

# LIFE ON THE FLOOD PLAINS

The muddy flood plains and sandy river banks of the late Jurassic teemed with life. Ferns, cycads, and horsetails growing thickly in the marshy areas made good hiding places for small animals. Moss-covered conifers, ginkgoes, seed ferns, and cycadeoids created thick forests. In places, the river was choked with rotting logs. The hot air was heavy with moisture, and insects were abundant. Primitive dragonflies swarmed in the air, as big and small beetles scurried in the undergrowth or flew from tree to tree.

## Plants

Jurassic plants were evergreen — they didn't shed their leaves, for the weather was always warm and heavy rains gave them plenty of water. Plants were evergreen and all green — flowers had not yet evolved.

## Fish

Although muddy, the wide river was still home to fish, clams, and snails. Lungfish could gulp air if the water became stagnant.

*Ophiopsis*

*Aspidorhynchus*

## Turtles

*Glyptops* hunted small fish, frogs, crayfish, and worms. Turtles also liked to eat soft water plants.

## Mammals

*Docodon* was a small shy mammal, with hair to keep it warm. It probably ate insects, worms, and seeds. It fed mostly at night, when there were fewer enemies about.

## Pterosaurs

Flying reptiles called pterosaurs challenged birds in the air. *Comodactylus*, and its cousin *Rhamphorhynchus*, could escape the dangers of the ground by using their wings.

## Lizards

Small reptiles scampered through the brush and hid in the trees, chasing insects and basking in the sun.

## Insects

Insect life was plentiful. Then, as now, they were more numerous than any other animal group. These are stoneflies.

# PEACEFUL NEIGHBORS

There were many dinosaurs in the world of *Stegosaurus*. Most were peaceful plant eaters, feeding on the rich foliage of the forest and flood plain. There were no grasses, so they ate low-growing shrubs, or browsed on the leaves and pine-like needles of tall trees. Long-necked sauropods, like *Diplodocus*, *Brachiosaurus*, and *Barosaurus*, could feed on the topmost branches. Smaller dinosaurs, like the ornithopods, preferred easier pickings nearer the ground. All ate huge amounts of vegetation and were constantly alert for signs of their enemies — the meat-eating theropods. Any sign of danger from a nearby predator might cause the plant eaters to stampede.

**Camptosaurus**

KAMP-toe-SAW-rus
"BENT REPTILE"
23 FT. (7 M) LONG

This common dinosaur walked on broad hooflike toes — either on two legs, or four.

**Dryosaurus**

DRY-oh-SAW-rus
"OAK REPTILE"
13 FT. (4 M) LONG

The heavy-horned beak of this ornithopod helped it bite through tough leaves and fronds.

## *Apatosaurus*

a-PAT-oh-SAW-rus
"DECEPTIVE REPTILE"
70 FT. (21 M) LONG

*Apatosaurus* is the best known of the sauropod group of dinosaurs.

# FRIGHTFUL FOES

Many animals kill and eat their neighbors for food. There were many large dinosaurs that were enemies of *Stegosaurus*. These meat-eating predators were the theropods. They all walked on two legs, like birds, and had pointed teeth for stabbing and cutting flesh. Paleontologists often find these pointed teeth with the bones of other dinosaurs — proof that they were eaten by theropods. All herbivorous (plant-eating) dinosaurs were at risk from carnivores (meat eaters). Some plant eaters, like the sauropods, traveled in tight herds to protect their young from theropod attack.

**Torvosaurus**

TOR-voh-SAW-rus
"SAVAGE REPTILE"
33 FT. (10 M) LONG

This rare theropod was as dangerous as *Allosaurus*.

**Ceratosaurus**

ser-AT-oh-SAW-rus
"HORNED REPTILE"
20 FT. (6 M) LONG

The horn on its snout may have been useful for frightening rivals.

**Ornitholestes**

or-NITH-oh-LESS-teez
"BIRD ROBBER"
6 FT. 6 IN. (2 M) LONG

This swift runner may have scavenged on dead animals, or stolen eggs and babies.

▼ *Allosaurus* must have been aggressive toward intruders. Threatening glances and a fierce roar might prevent a fight with an outsider.

### *Allosaurus*
AL-oh-SAW-rus
"OTHER REPTILE"
36 FT. (11 M) LONG

The late Jurassic theropod *Allosaurus* was a ferocious hunter and killer. It could easily eat a large plant eater. It tore off big chunks of meat with its sharp teeth and swallowed them whole.

# THE ROOFED REPTILE

*Stegosaurus* is an easily recognized dinosaur, because of its set of back plates. These were large and flat, and projected up from the spine. Its tail spikes are another trademark. Scientists have reconstructed *Stegosaurus*, like most dinosaurs, from single bones and mixed-up skeletons. Paleontology is like a detective story and 3-D jigsaw puzzle rolled into one. It can take years for the bony clues to be dug up, studied, and pieced into a complete animal. It's hard work, but without it, no one would have heard of dinosaurs today. In fact, the word *dinosaur* was first used only 150 years ago. Since then, several hundred species of dinosaur have been discovered.

▶ The paleontologist must imagine the living appearance of a dinosaur. He models its muscles after living animals. Fossil impressions of dinosaur skin show that it was rough and pebbly, almost like an alligator's. The plates of *Stegosaurus* were made thicker by their horny covering.

▶ The bones of *Stegosaurus* show that it had a very small head and a large body. The front legs were much shorter than the back ones, so maybe *Stegosaurus* had an ancestor that walked on its hind legs. *Stegosaurus* had broad feet that gave support to the heavy, bulky body. The tail ended in a spray of spikes.

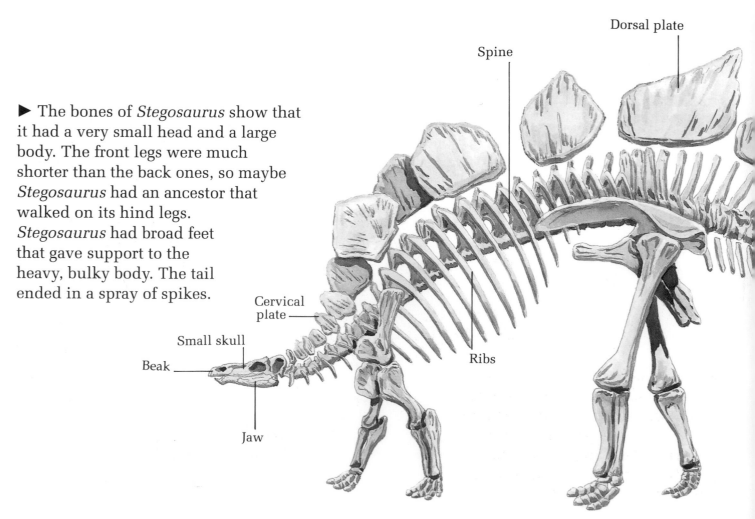

Spine

Dorsal plate

Cervical plate

Small skull

Beak

Jaw

Ribs

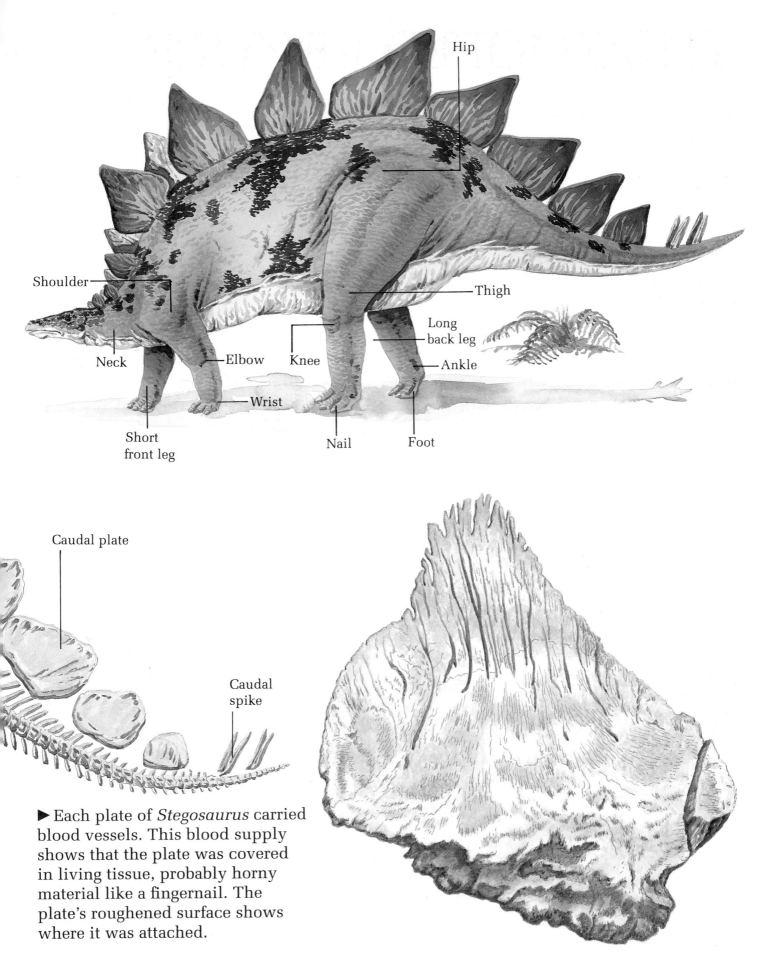

Hip

Shoulder

Neck

Elbow

Knee

Wrist

Short
front leg

Nail

Foot

Ankle

Long
back leg

Thigh

Caudal plate

Caudal
spike

▶ Each plate of *Stegosaurus* carried
blood vessels. This blood supply
shows that the plate was covered
in living tissue, probably horny
material like a fingernail. The
plate's roughened surface shows
where it was attached.

# PROBLEMS OF THE PLATES

*Stegosaurus* plates were unusual things — even for a dinosaur. They were tall and thin, and planted in the skin and muscles of its back, not attached to the backbones. It is therefore hard to know exactly where they belong. Paleontologists have had to use guesswork for the plate positions when reconstructing this dinosaur. Several different ideas about their placement, as well as their use, have been suggested. Even today, not everyone agrees about stegosaur plates and spines. Some scientists believe that the plates were used to control the body temperature of *Stegosaurus*, but we can never be certain. Most scientists think that the plates were a type of armor.

▼ If *Stegosaurus* was too hot, the theory of temperature control says that it moved its plates out of the sun, into the shade or wind.

▲ By basking in the morning sun, a stegosaur might pick up heat with its plates, if the blood in them flowed to a covering of skin.

## ELEPHANT EARS

The big ears are not to hear with, but to keep cool in the sun. When they flap in the breeze, the blood in the skin is cooled (like *Stegosaurus* plates?).

▲ Posture and position are the biggest problems of the plates. An early idea was that they lay flat on the back. We don't think this is right, because the plates are the wrong shape.

▶ The plates probably stood upright. Most people think they were in two rows, but were they side-by-side or alternating? There is no way to tell unless a perfect skeleton is found.

◀ A new theory is that alternate rows of plates at the front of *Stegosaurus* became a single row at the back. There were not enough plates for two complete rows.

# A DEFENSIVE DRAMA

Probably the best explanation for the plates of *Stegosaurus*, is that they were protection from big theropod predators. It would certainly be difficult to bite into a stegosaur's back. The tail, with its four great horny spikes, was probably a "war club" to fend off attackers. Unlike most ornithischian dinosaurs, *Stegosaurus* had no bony rods running along its tail. This means that the tail was especially flexible, and so could be swung against an enemy. A blow from this spiky tail would inflict a horrible wound. A hungry theropod might therefore look elsewhere for its next meal.

▶ *Stegosaurus* must have turned its back and tail toward any advancing threat. Feet firmly planted on the ground, the tail hovered menacingly in the face of danger, *Stegosaurus* would keep a watchful eye on its foe. The horn covering the plates was probably sharp too!

## STEGOSAUR COLORS

Different colors attract mates, provide camouflage, or confuse enemies. Maybe large, brightly colored stegosaur plates were used for display, like the frills of some lizards.

Frilled lizard

## AGGRESSIVE *ALLOSAURUS*

Predators, such as *Allosaurus*, were wary of the business end of *Stegosaurus*. They had to maneuver around an alert *Stegosaurus*, and try and attack its unprotected sides.

# MAKING A LIVING

The bones and teeth of *Stegosaurus* give us many clues about its life. It is the job of the paleontologist to put these clues together. We think that the armor plates and spines were for defense, or perhaps display. What do the other bones of *Stegosaurus* tell us? The teeth show that it was a vegetarian, and since the position of its head was so low to the ground, *Stegosaurus* must have eaten mostly low-growing plants. *Stegosaurus* had to eat and drink, but also give birth to young stegosaurs. Like the babies of other dinosaurs, its young probably hatched out of eggs. Some dinosaurs apparently cared for their little ones; it is likely that *Stegosaurus* brought food to babies too young to leave their nests.

## BROWSING

*Stegosaurus* might have reached fresh, higher leaves by rearing up on its back legs and tail.

## YOUNG AND GROWN-UPS

*Stegosaurus* used its sharp, horny beak to cut up plant food, such as ferns. Its baby did the same soon after birth, for it needed lots of food to grow quickly. It was a miniature version of its mother, but had much smaller plates and spines. These grew larger with age.

▶ Some dinosaurs made nests in the soil, which they covered with rotting vegetation. This kept the eggs warm. *Stegosaurus* laid its eggs in a place safe from danger — away from floods, egg eaters, and the feet of other dinosaurs.

## FOOD SUPPLY

*Stegosaurus* had plenty to eat when the rains came. Did it migrate to greener pastures during the periodic drought?

## STEGOSAUR TEETH

Stegosaur teeth were very small and weak. *Stegosaurus, Kentrosaurus,* and *Tuojiangosaurus* could only chew soft plants. Perhaps they swallowed stones to help their stomachs grind up tougher meals.

# STEGOSAUR COUSINS

*Stegosaurus* was only one of many different plated dinosaurs. The Stegosauria flourished in the Jurassic and lived in many parts of the world. The earliest complete stegosaur is *Huayangosaurus* from the middle Jurassic of China, but early stegosaur bones and teeth are also found in Europe. Cretaceous stegosaurs are rare — there are only bits from England, South Africa, and China. The last stegosaur was *Dravidosaurus* from the late Cretaceous of India. Perhaps stegosaurs were made obsolete by their more heavily armored cousins, the ankylosaurs.

▼ *Stegosaurus*, from the late Jurassic of North America, is the best known, and one of the largest, stegosaurs. It also had the biggest plates of any known stegosaur.

| ***Stegosaurus*** |
| :---: |
| STEG-oh-SAW-rus |
| "ROOFED REPTILE" |
| 30 FT. (9 M) LONG |

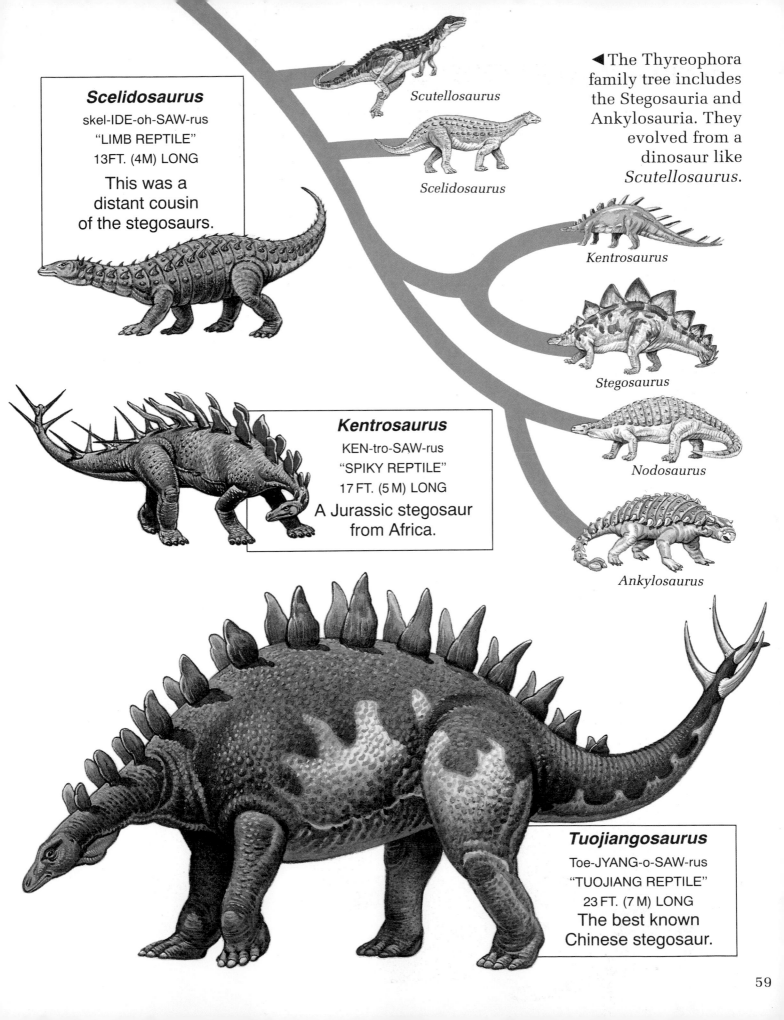

**Scelidosaurus**

skel-IDE-oh-SAW-rus
"LIMB REPTILE"
13FT. (4M) LONG

This was a distant cousin of the stegosaurs.

*Scutellosaurus*

*Scelidosaurus*

◄ The Thyreophora family tree includes the Stegosauria and Ankylosauria. They evolved from a dinosaur like *Scutellosaurus*.

*Kentrosaurus*

*Stegosaurus*

*Nodosaurus*

*Ankylosaurus*

**Kentrosaurus**

KEN-tro-SAW-rus
"SPIKY REPTILE"
17 FT. (5 M) LONG

A Jurassic stegosaur from Africa.

**Tuojiangosaurus**

Toe-JYANG-o-SAW-rus
"TUOJIANG REPTILE"
23 FT. (7 M) LONG
The best known Chinese stegosaur.

# DINOSAUR BRAINS

*Stegosaurus* had a very small brain for its large body — about the size of a doorknob. Obviously, *Stegosaurus* was not very clever, but it was a successful animal, so its brain was big enough for its needs. Even a small brain is a very complex organ. Dinosaur brains can be studied from the petrified sediment fillings of their skulls, or, if the skull is hollow, an artificial rubber mold. The size and shape of the braincase and positions of nerves can be seen in this way. Braincase fossils, called endocasts, show us that most dinosaurs probably acted more like modern reptiles or birds than mammals, relying on keen senses and instinct, instead of intelligence. The *Stegosaurus* brain was one of the first dinosaur brains to be studied. Even today, the study of fossil brains, called paleoneurology, can give us important clues about the behavior of extinct animals.

## A SECOND BRAIN?

The hip of *Stegosaurus* had a large space for the spinal cord, giving rise to the myth that it had two brains. In fact, it housed a nerve swelling, called a spinal plexus.

▶ The spinal plexus of the hip cavity was a spot where many nerves met. All vertebrates have a similar nerve swelling. A new theory suggests that the space also held a gland, called a glycogen body, that gave extra energy in times of stress.

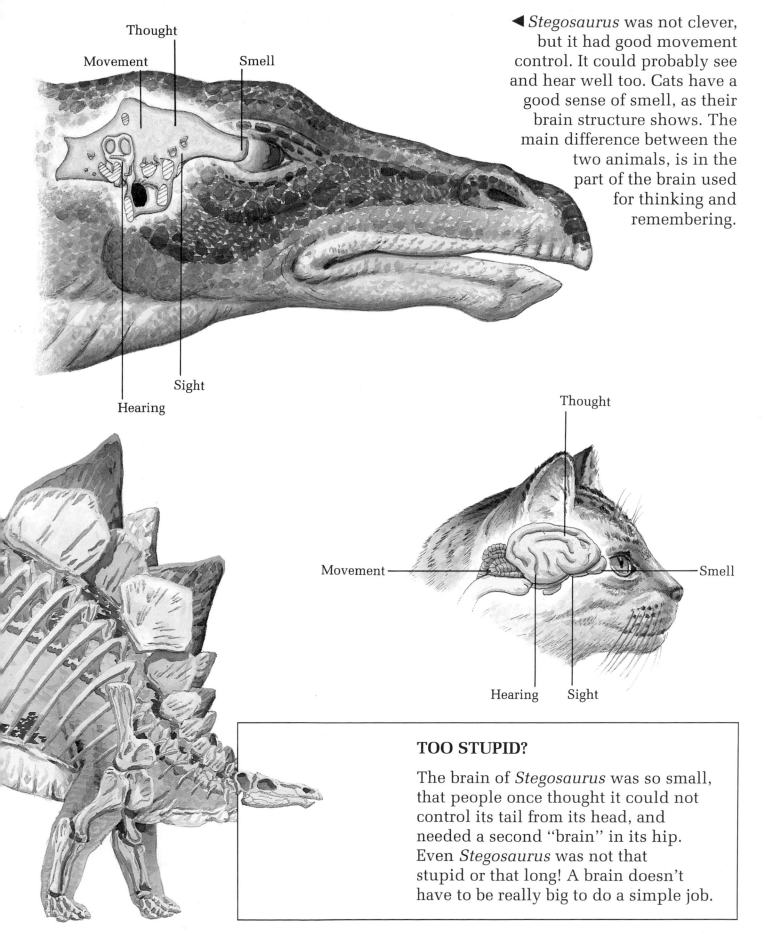

Thought

Movement

Smell

Sight

Hearing

◄ *Stegosaurus* was not clever, but it had good movement control. It could probably see and hear well too. Cats have a good sense of smell, as their brain structure shows. The main difference between the two animals, is in the part of the brain used for thinking and remembering.

Thought

Movement

Smell

Hearing

Sight

## TOO STUPID?

The brain of *Stegosaurus* was so small, that people once thought it could not control its tail from its head, and needed a second "brain" in its hip. Even *Stegosaurus* was not that stupid or that long! A brain doesn't have to be really big to do a simple job.

# DINOFACTS

**Q**: How long did *Stegosaurus* live?

**A**: Most dinosaurs probably lived to be quite old. Modern turtles may live to over one hundred years, and may grow all during their life. Perhaps very large dinosaurs were just as long-lived. Some dinosaur bones and teeth show growth layers, like the yearly rings in a tree trunk. We might guess how quickly and how long these dinosaurs grew from evidence like this. On the other hand, many dinosaur bones do not have growth rings, but are like those in fast-growing animals. Maybe dinosaurs like *Stegosaurus* grew to a large size quickly, but still lived a long time.

**Q**: Was *Stegosaurus* slimy?

**A**: No. Like all reptiles, including snakes, *Stegosaurus* had dry, scaly skin. Because reptiles live mainly on land, they must protect themselves from drying out. The tough scaly skin keeps the body's water in. We also know from the preserved skin impressions of other dinosaurs, that the skin of *Stegosaurus* was probably rough with large, horny scales covering it.

▶ Rare mummified dinosaurs, like this *Edmontosaurus*, preserve the texture of dinosaur skin. The skin was fossilized by hot, dry sand.

**Q**: How fast was *Stegosaurus*?

**A**: We don't know, but we can guess. Some dinosaurs have left behind fossil footprints that tell us how they moved. By measuring the distance between the prints, and comparing the length of the leg, we can judge a dinosaur's speed. Sadly, no *Stegosaurus* tracks are known. As the stout limbs of *Stegosaurus* were obviously not built for speed, they probably walked slowly most of the time. *Stegosaurus* did not need to run from its enemies — it was protected by its "war club" tail and defensive plates.

**Q**: How can you tell the difference between a male and female *Stegosaurus*?

**A**: The sex of fossils is very difficult, if not impossible, to determine. However, just as in most modern reptiles and birds, a female dinosaur may have been larger than the male of the same species. Maybe a very large *Stegosaurus* was a female. The sexes of some animals are shown in their different colors and shapes. With most deer, a stag has antlers but a doe does not. Perhaps the plates and spikes of *Stegosaurus* were slightly different in males and females.

Red deer

**Q**: Why did the stegosaurs become extinct?

**A**: No one knows why they died out. They seem to have been one of the first major groups of dinosaurs to become extinct, and were not part of the "mass extinction" at the end of the Cretaceous age (although the last known stegosaur, *Dravidosaurus*, is from the late Cretaceous of India). Perhaps stegosaurs could not keep up with a changing climate. Maybe, they fell prey to disease, or were out-competed by fitter dinosaurs. If an asteroid killed the dinosaurs at the end of the Cretaceous, this was long after the stegosaurs had gone. Did the giant dinosaurs become extinct through accident, or changing conditions?

**Q**: Will we ever know more about how *Stegosaurus* lived?

**A**: We hope so. A new *Stegosaurus* skeleton was recently discovered in Colorado. It may be the best fossil ever found of this dinosaur, and should help to answer some of the questions that still puzzle us about *Stegosaurus*. It is now being studied by scientists at the Denver Museum of Natural History.

▶ The "mass extinction" at the end of the Cretaceous is one of the great unsolved mysteries of nature.

# FINDING *STEGOSAURUS*

*Stegosaurus* bones are found in the colorful rocks of the Morrison Formation of the western United States. A famous site is at Como Bluff, Wyoming. Tons of dinosaur fossils have been collected here and sent to museums around the world. Professor Othniel C. Marsh of Yale College led teams of students to the American West in the 1870s. His men collected bones of *Stegosaurus*, and other late Jurassic dinosaurs, from a number of dinosaur graveyards, including Como Bluff. Marsh created a sensation by reconstructing the appearance of many of these giant dinosaurs. He also named more new dinosaur species than anyone else.

◄The great American "dinosaur rush" took place when the West was still wild. Marsh is pictured here with a geological hammer, but his students have rifles!

►The paintings of Arthur Lakes give us a good idea of conditions at the "digs." One painting shows men collecting in a snowstorm!

▶ The first reconstruction of *Stegosaurus* was made by Marsh in 1891. This had one row of plates and too many spikes, but even in the 1890s the basic features were plain.

▼ Como Bluff is badland country with gullies and few plants. There is little rain. Paleontologists prefer to look for fossils in places like this, where the rocks are easy to examine and are not hidden by forests or cities! Of course, the rocks must be of the right age.

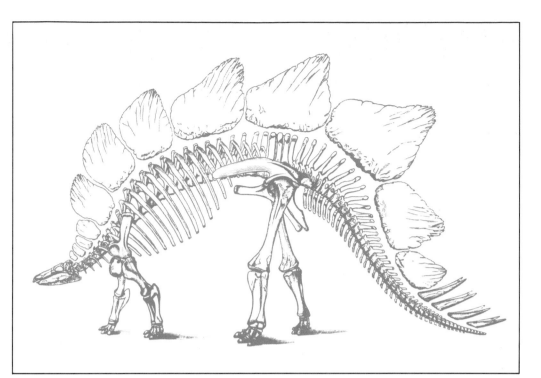

# The World of Deinonychus

## *Period: Early Cretaceous— 110 million years ago*

Just when you thought that *Tyrannosaurus* was the most frightening dinosaur, *Deinonychus* rears its fearsome head. Unlike the gigantic tyrant king, however, *Deinonychus* was a small dinosaur, not much longer than 10 or 12 feet. Like other meat eaters, though, it had a mouth full of sharp, pointed teeth for cutting into flesh. Add to that the sharp claws at the ends of the fingers and you have a formidable predator. But what made this dinosaur much more frightening than any other meat eater of its time was the huge savage claw on the second toe of each foot. In fact, *Deinonychus* was given its name (meaning "terrible claw") because of the whopping big can openers on its toes! With great agility, *Deinonychus* would bound after its prey, striking at it with its razor-sharp hind feet, and then ripping and tearing until the animal was dead. To make matters worse, *Deinonychus* was quite intelligent by dinosaur standards. Probably hunting in packs, these animals may have used their intelligence to track their prey, working out the best time to make their move. When these deadly hunters were around, there wasn't much chance for any other dinosaur that *Deinonychus* chose to chase.

Where did all this information and these ideas about *Deinonychus* come from? None of it had even been guessed at 30 years ago, when this important dinosaur was discovered. It took dinosaur hunter John Ostrom and other scientists to piece together the puzzle of the sickle-clawed dinosaur. His discoveries in the wilds of Wyoming and Montana made scientists realize that dinosaurs were far from being slow and dim-witted failures, but rather the most active and clever successes of their times! The discovery of *Deinonychus* also made people realize that while *Tyrannosaurus* may have been the largest meat-eater of all time, *Deinonychus* has got to be the scariest! The pages that follow show how we came to learn all this—and more—about the Terrible Claw.

**David B. Weishampel**
*Associate Professor*
Johns Hopkins University

# *DEINONYCHUS* TIMELINE

Dinosaurs lived on Earth for about 165 million years. But *Deinonychus* was only around for part of the Dinosaur Age — sometime during the 50-million-year interval called the early Cretaceous. This was an important time in dinosaur evolution. Earlier periods had been dominated by giant plant-eating dinosaurs such as *Brachiosaurus*. But by the early Cretaceous, the chief plant eaters were two-legged dinosaurs such as *Iguanodon*. Other species included meat eaters such as *Baryonyx*, as well as armored, plant-eating dinosaurs such as *Sauropelta*.

*Tenontosaurus*

*Baryonyx*

*Deinonychus*

*Ornitholestes*

*Glyptops*

*Microvenator*

LATE TRIASSIC

JURASSIC

| | | | Early | | Middle | |
|---|---|---|---|---|---|---|

Millions of Years Ago

| 230 | 220 | 210 | 200 | 190 | 180 | 170 | 160 |

*Pterodactylus*

*Iguanodon*

▼ Typical early Cretaceous dinosaurs included the meat eaters *Deinonychus* and *Baryonyx*. Although different in many ways, they both had big slashing claws. Two-legged plant eaters included *Iguanodon* and *Hypsilophodon*, a close relative of *Tenontosaurus*, a prey of *Deinonychus*. There were also ankylosaurs, such as *Sauropelta*, as well as turtles, pterosaurs, and crocodiles.

*Hypsilophodon*

*Sauropelta*

*Goniopholis*

▼ Life on Earth is measured in millions of years, divided up into units. Dinosaurs lived during the Mesozoic era, which is divided into three periods, the Triassic, Jurassic, and Cretaceous. Dinosaurs lived from the late Triassic to the end of the Cretaceous.

CRETACEOUS

| Early | Late |

145    130    120    110    100    95    90    80    70    65

# 110 MILLION YEARS AGO

When *Deinonychus* was alive, a map of the world looked quite different from a map of today's world. This is because the continents and oceans have been moving slowly sideways for millions of years. At that time, the world had a tropical climate, with plenty of rain. As it was warm as far north and as far south as the polar regions, dinosaurs had a wider range than modern reptiles.

▼ In Cretaceous times there was only a bit of the Atlantic Ocean between North America and Africa. The coastlines of parts of present-day America and Europe were covered by seas. The probable position of some mountain ranges are shown on the map.

LAURASIA

GONDWANALAND

1. *Deinonychus*

2. *Velociraptor*

3. *Dromaeosaurus*

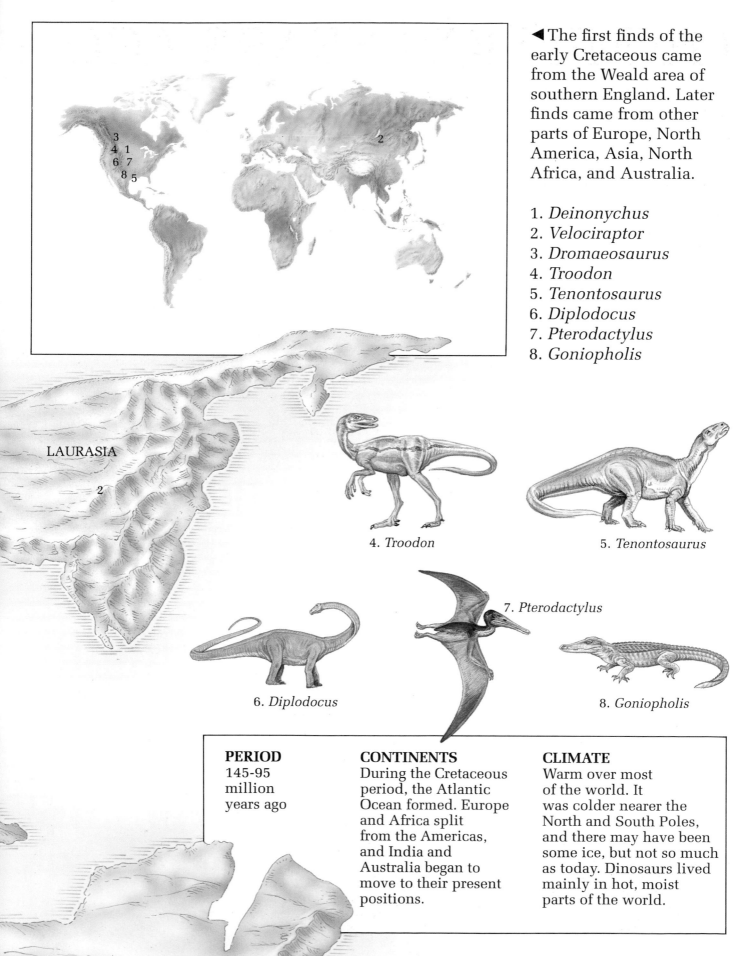

◄ The first finds of the early Cretaceous came from the Weald area of southern England. Later finds came from other parts of Europe, North America, Asia, North Africa, and Australia.

1. *Deinonychus*
2. *Velociraptor*
3. *Dromaeosaurus*
4. *Troodon*
5. *Tenontosaurus*
6. *Diplodocus*
7. *Pterodactylus*
8. *Goniopholis*

LAURASIA

4. *Troodon*

5. *Tenontosaurus*

7. *Pterodactylus*

6. *Diplodocus*

8. *Goniopholis*

**PERIOD**
145-95 million years ago

**CONTINENTS**
During the Cretaceous period, the Atlantic Ocean formed. Europe and Africa split from the Americas, and India and Australia began to move to their present positions.

**CLIMATE**
Warm over most of the world. It was colder nearer the North and South Poles, and there may have been some ice, but not so much as today. Dinosaurs lived mainly in hot, moist parts of the world.

# THE MONTANA BADLANDS

*Deinonychus*'s world was quite different from present-day Montana, where its remains were found. About 110 million years ago, this semidesert was subtropical lowland. Cycads, ferns, and horsetails supplied food for plant-eating dinosaurs. Dragonflies and other insects flew over pools, which were full of fish and snails.

▶ The cannonball-like cycads, and the ferns and horsetails, were all larger, more primitive versions of modern plants.

▶ Dragonflies are some of the most primitive insects. They have two pairs of wings that flap with different timing. Some of the prehistoric dragonflies were very large.

▶ A plant-eating *Tenontosaurus* watches the pack of *Deinonychus* chasing one of its herd.

▼ *Deinonychus* lived in a low-lying, lightly forested region, crossed by rivers and freshwater pools. The higher land roughly followed the line of the modern Rocky Mountain range.

◄ Pterosaurs were rare in Montana in the early Cretaceous, although a few could probably be seen diving into ponds to seize a fish.

◄ Prehistoric crocodiles patrolled the rivers. Other water life included snails, fish, freshwater clams, and insect larvae.

▲ A pack of *Deinonychus* race off in pursuit of a plant eater they have been tracking.

◄ Small mammals were mainly nocturnal, tree-climbing insect eaters. A treelike cycad was a good hiding place for a small mammal.

# ANIMALS OF THE BADLANDS

It is fun to work out what dinosaurs ate. It is also fun to work out what ate dinosaurs. It seems likely that *Deinonychus* had no real enemies, as no giant meat eaters have been found in Montana. However, many other plants and animals lived on the land, and in the ponds and lakes. These may give clues about some of the things that *Deinonychus* ate. Fossil bones of fish, turtles, and crocodiles have been found with *Deinonychus*, while plants, shells, insects, pterosaurs, and early mammals have been found in nearby rocks of the same age.

## Land Plants

When *Deinonychus* lived, the tallest trees were conifers, trees similar to modern pines and firs. There may have been a few flowers, but there was no grass.

## Early Mammals

Mammals were the size of rats or mice; they fed mainly on insects.

## Crocodiles

*Goniopholis*, a large crocodile, is munching a flat-shelled turtle, like a bony hamburger.

## Turtles

The large freshwater turtle *Glytops* probably lived in ponds, where it hunted small fish.

Water beetle

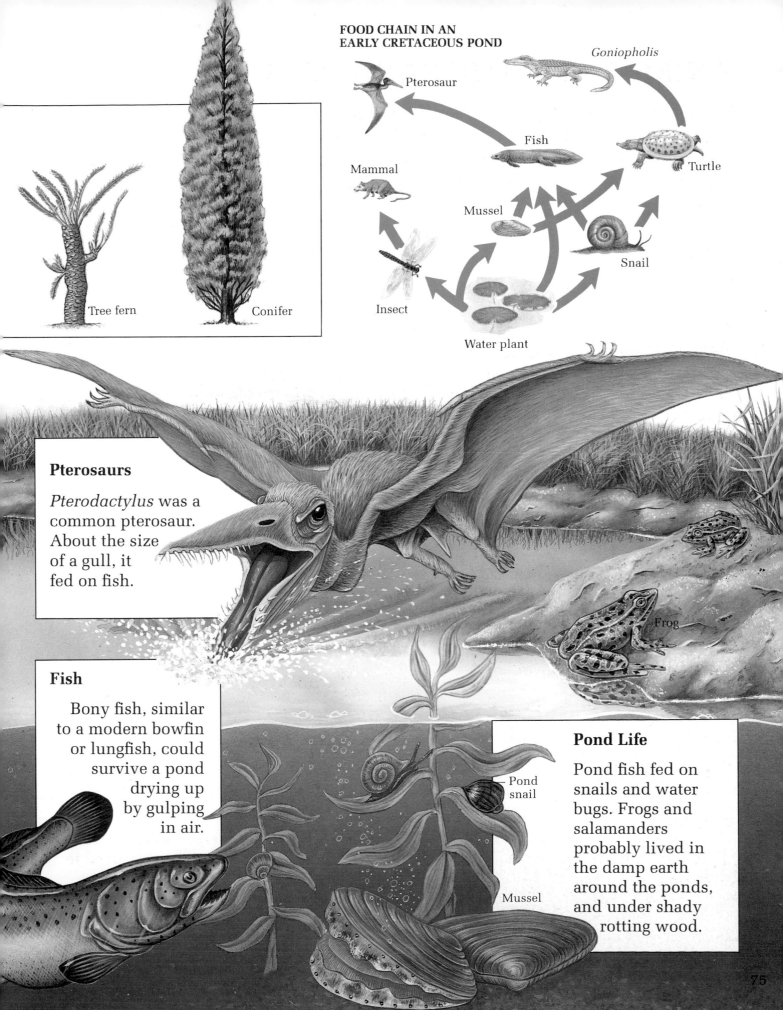

## FOOD CHAIN IN AN EARLY CRETACEOUS POND

Tree fern

Conifer

Pterosaur

*Goniopholis*

Fish

Turtle

Mammal

Mussel

Snail

Insect

Water plant

## Pterosaurs

*Pterodactylus* was a common pterosaur. About the size of a gull, it fed on fish.

Frog

## Fish

Bony fish, similar to a modern bowfin or lungfish, could survive a pond drying up by gulping in air.

Pond snail

Mussel

## Pond Life

Pond fish fed on snails and water bugs. Frogs and salamanders probably lived in the damp earth around the ponds, and under shady rotting wood.

75

# PREY

Although *Deinonychus* was not large, it was capable of attacking any other early Cretaceous dinosaur. Even bigger dinosaurs, such as the plant eater *Tenontosaurus*, was part of *Deinonychus*'s diet. *Tenontosaurus* was the most common dinosaur in Montana in early Cretaceous times. Its neighbors included the giant sauropod *Diplodocus*, and the armored ankylosaur *Sauropelta*. There were also some smaller meat-eating dinosaurs, living side-by-side with *Deinonychus*, that may have stolen eggs and baby dinosaurs from the nests of the plant eaters.

▼ The mother dinosaur laid up to 20 eggs in a shallow nest. After the babies had hatched, adults brought them leaves until they could feed themselves. The parents had to keep watch because small meat eaters were often waiting to snatch their helpless babies!

### Microvenator
MIKE-roe-ven-AH-tor
"SMALL HUNTER"
4 FT. (1.2 M) LONG

*Microvenator* was a sneaky little dinosaur that may have robbed nests.

## Tenontosaurus

Ten-ONT-oh-SAW-rus
"SINEW REPTILE"
15-21 FT. (4.5-6.5 M) LONG

It is likely that these gigantic plant eaters moved around together in search of food. This helped to protect them from attack.

## Sauropelta

SAW-roh-PEL-ta
"SHIELDED REPTILE"
20 FT. (7 M) LONG

A heavily armored dinosaur that belonged to the nodosaurid family of ankylosaurs.

## Diplodocus

Dip-LOD-oh-kus
"DOUBLE BEAM"
100 FT. (30 M) LONG

This four-legged plant eater had an amazingly long neck and tail.

# THE KILLER CLAW

*Deinonychus* was a terrifying killing machine whose body was designed for maximum speed and agility. Besides being able to run very fast, it also had a complete range of body weapons. It had a strong, lightly built skull, with tearing teeth. It also had a razor-sharp claw on each finger and toe. But its greatest weapon was the scythelike, 5-inch (12-centimeter)-long, "terrible claw" on the second toe of its back foot. This huge claw had a large bony core, which would have been covered by an even longer horny talon. When *Deinonychus* walked, it held the slashing claw up in a resting position. Some people have suggested that *Deinonychus* might have had feathers, but this is unlikely.

### Deinonychus

DIE-no-NIKE-US
"TERRIBLE CLAW"
12 FT. (4 M) LONG

The nearly complete fossil of this agile predator was one of the most exciting dinosaur discoveries of the 1960s.

ARC OF "TERRIBLE CLAW"

Bony rods to hold tail straight

**DEINONYCHUS FOOT AND CLAW**

Foot

Claw in resting position

Toe

◀ When *Deinonychus* attacked, it raised its foot, as it leaped through the air. It then swung its back leg down, while bringing its claw over faster than the eye could see. It was capable of ripping a yard-long wound in the side of its victim.

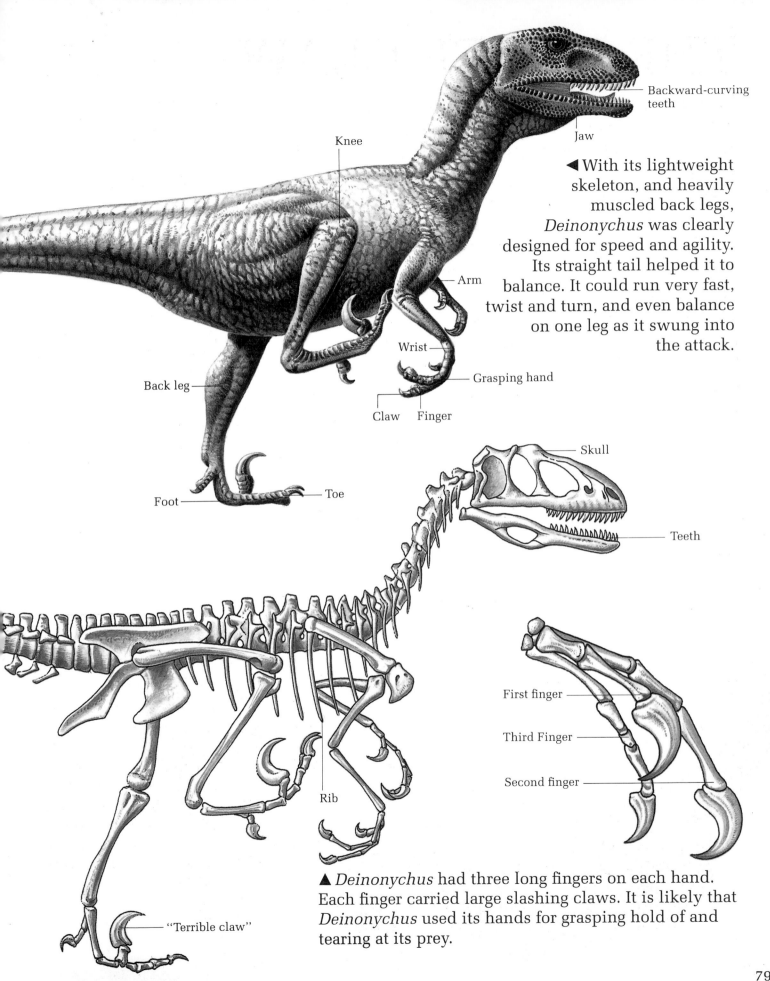

Backward-curving teeth

Jaw

Knee

◄ With its lightweight skeleton, and heavily muscled back legs, *Deinonychus* was clearly designed for speed and agility. Its straight tail helped it to balance. It could run very fast, twist and turn, and even balance on one leg as it swung into the attack.

Arm

Wrist

Grasping hand

Back leg

Claw    Finger

Skull

Teeth

Foot    Toe

First finger

Third Finger

Second finger

Rib

▲ *Deinonychus* had three long fingers on each hand. Each finger carried large slashing claws. It is likely that *Deinonychus* used its hands for grasping hold of and tearing at its prey.

"Terrible claw"

79

# KILLER INSTINCTS

Dinosaurs were usually not very clever, but *Deinonychus* may have been an exception. Because of the speed with which it attacked its prey, *Deinonychus* had to be able to think quickly. Its big brain also indicates exceptionally good eyesight. Like its relation *Troodon*, *Deinonychus* may also have had forward-facing eyes. Most dinosaurs were like the majority of modern animals, and saw a different scene with each eye. That is why a horse or a duck shakes its head from side to side when it comes up to you.

◀ When *Deinonychus* attacked, it balanced on one leg, moved forward, turned rapidly, and swung down with its claw.

▼ *Deinonychus* probably had a top speed of about 20 miles (35 km) an hour. This is about the same as the top speed of an ostrich or a racehorse.

Brain   Eyes

Ears

Nostrils

◀ This *Deinonychus* has such a hungry look in its eyes that it has probably just spotted a tasty looking plant eater. Predatory dinosaurs such as *Deinonychus* needed good eyesight to catch their prey. Like other dinosaurs, it did not have external ears, but heard through passages in the back of its skull.

Field of vision

*Deinonychus*                    Owl

## SPECIALIZED SIGHT

*Deinonychus* may have had binocular vision (forward-facing eyes). This type of vision gives modern birds, such as eagles and owls, a single view of an object, and helps them judge the distance of their prey. Dinosaurs with eyes on the side of their heads had a double view of objects.

# PACK AND ATTACK

A big game hunter, *Deinonychus* was probably also a top team player. The prey of this dinosaur almost certainly included larger dinosaurs, such as *Tenontosaurus*, and giants such as *Diplodocus*. It is possible that *Deinonychus* only ate smaller dinosaurs. It may also have hunted alone, as some big cats do, killing a larger animal by biting or slashing at its neck. However, it is more likely that *Deinonychus* was clever enough to work out a game plan of hunting in swift-moving killer packs.

▼ *Deinonychus*'s favorite meal was probably *Tenontosaurus*. However, as *Tenontosaurus* was six times larger than its attackers, it would have taken four or five *Deinonychus* to kill one of these monsters. The pack's plan would have been to leap at its prey, and slash *Tenontosaurus*'s sides with their claws.

▼ With their body armor of bony back plates and spines, the ankylosaurs could usually protect themselves from attack. A further defensive measure was for an ankylosaur to crouch close to the ground, like a turtle. However, if two or three *Deinonychus* pulled an ankylosaur such as *Sauropelta* onto its back, they could then slash at its unprotected underside.

## PACK ANIMALS

Hunting dogs and wolves are modern animals that hunt in packs. Each pack has a leader, and everyone in the pack has a job to do. The pack selects a victim and separates it from the rest of the herd. It then chases the victim, until it is exhausted, and can be dragged down and killed.

▶ Because of their size, *Deinonychus* would have found fully grown sauropods, such as *Diplodocus*, the most difficult prey to kill. In the picture, the killer pack has chosen to attack a young *Diplodocus* that has become separated from its family group. Four *Deinonychus* are about to close in on the doomed youngster.

# A FAMILY CIRCLE

*Deinonychus* was a member of a fearsome group of meat-eating dinosaurs called the Deinonychosauria. The dinosaurs in this group are easily recognized by the large slashing claw on the second toe of each foot. There were at least two deinonychosaur families. The Dromaeosauridae includes medium-sized predators such as *Deinonychus*, *Dromaeosaurus*, and *Velociraptor*. The Saurornithoididae includes lightly built predators such as *Troodon*, and possibly larger dinosaurs, such as *Deinocheirus*.

▲ So far, the only parts of *Deinocheirus* that have been found are its amazing arms. Until more bones are found, we can only guess that the arms belonged to a giant flesh eater.

**Dromaeosaurus**
DROME-ee-oh-SAW-rus
"RUNNING REPTILE"
6 FT. (1.8 M) LONG

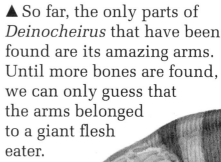

**Troodon**
Tro-o-don
"WOUNDING TOOTH"
6 FT. (2 M) LONG

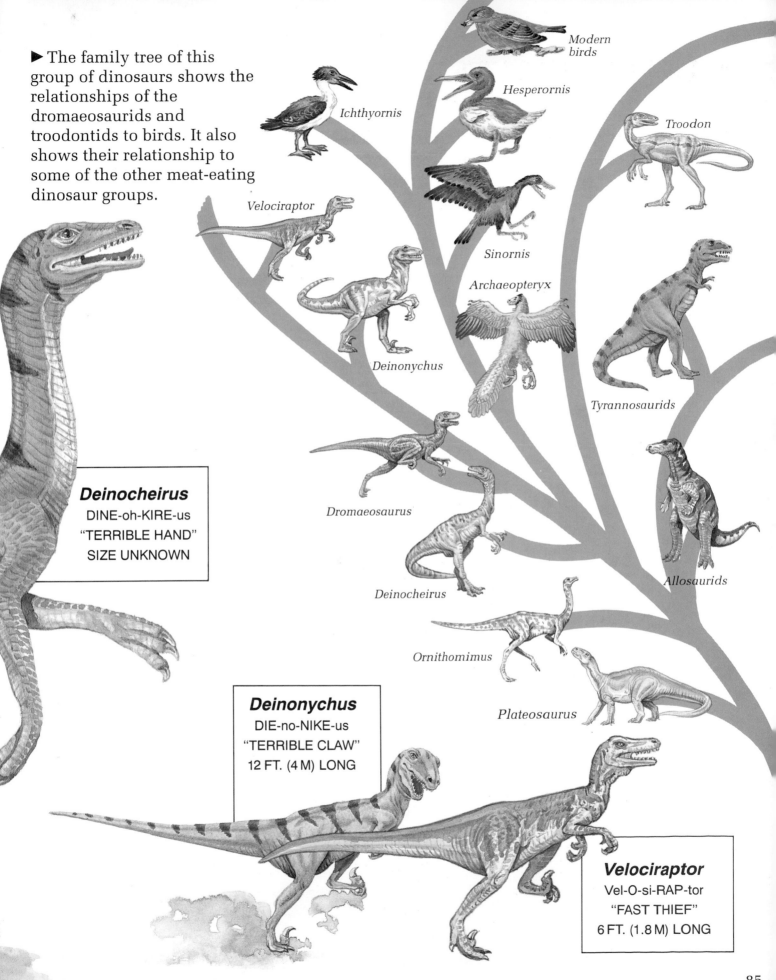

► The family tree of this group of dinosaurs shows the relationships of the dromaeosaurids and troodontids to birds. It also shows their relationship to some of the other meat-eating dinosaur groups.

Modern birds

Hesperornis

*Ichthyornis*

Troodon

*Velociraptor*

*Sinornis*

*Archaeopteryx*

*Deinonychus*

Tyrannosaurids

*Dromaeosaurus*

*Deinocheirus*

Allosaurids

*Ornithomimus*

*Plateosaurus*

**Deinocheirus**
DINE-oh-KIRE-us
"TERRIBLE HAND"
SIZE UNKNOWN

**Deinonychus**
DIE-no-NIKE-us
"TERRIBLE CLAW"
12 FT. (4 M) LONG

**Velociraptor**
Vel-O-si-RAP-tor
"FAST THIEF"
6 FT. (1.8 M) LONG

# A DEADLY CONTEST

In 1971, a remarkable fossil of two dinosaurs fighting was dug up in Mongolia. A *Velociraptor* was caught fighting a *Protoceratops*, a small plant-eating horned dinosaur. *Protoceratops* was one of the first horned dinosaurs, a group that later included the giant *Triceratops*. In early Cretaceous Mongolia, large numbers of *Protoceratops* fed on the tough low plants. In the 1920s, a number of *Protoceratops* nests were dug up and fossil babies were found. Perhaps this *Velociraptor* was trying to rob the *Protoceratops* nest, and the mother or father came to fight off the attacker.

▼ Although it was more lightly built than *Deinonychus*, *Velociraptor* was just as deadly. However, on at least one occasion, it was obviously not strong enough to overcome a heavily armored plant eater, such as *Protoceratops*.

**Protoceratops**
Pro-toe-SER-a-tops
"FIRST HORNED FACE"
6 FT. (1.8 M) LONG

*Protoceratops* had no horns but a pointed beak and a head shield.

▼ The fossil remains of two dinosaurs locked in combat. *Velociraptor* seems to be gripping the head shield of *Protoceratops*, while lashing with its giant claw. At the same time, *Protoceratops* has pierced *Velociraptor*'s chest.

# DEINONYCHUS AND BIRDS

Birds are living dinosaurs. When the first fossil of *Archaeopteryx* was found in Germany, in 1861, it appeared to be a reptile skeleton with a bird's feathers. Amazingly, the prints of the feathers were to be seen in the limestone around the bones. These feathers were very like those of living birds. Here was a "missing link" between reptiles and birds! It has now been proved that *Deinonychus* is one of the closest dinosaur relatives of birds.

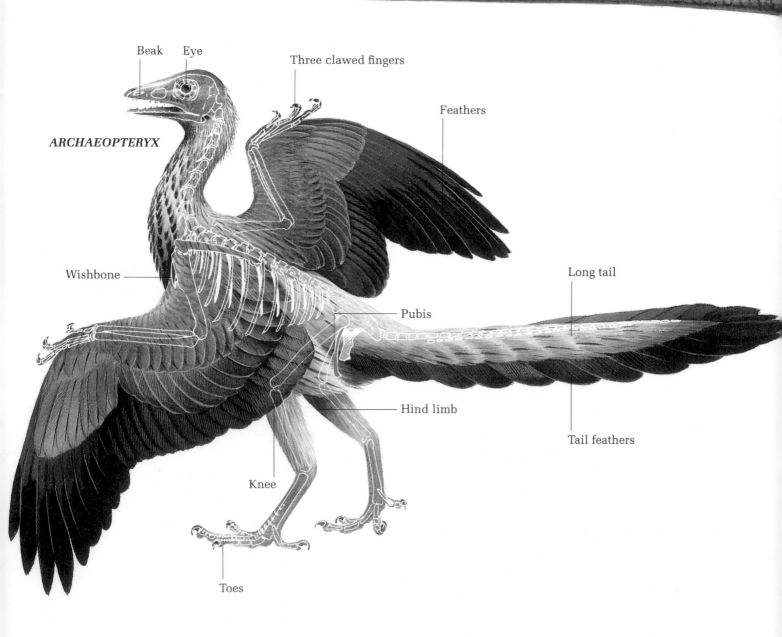

Long tail

**ARCHAEOPTERYX**

Beak

Eye

Three clawed fingers

Feathers

Wishbone

Pubis

Long tail

Hind limb

Tail feathers

Knee

Toes

Neck

Pubis    Knee    Elbow

Wishbone

Hind limb

Forelimb    Clawed fingers

Ankle

Toes

Foot

**PIGEON**

Beak

Wishbone

Wing

Tail    Pubis    Claws

▲ *Deinonychus* is very like the early birds. Its light skull and short backward-curved teeth are nearly the same. The three-toed feet are also the same, although birds do not have a slashing claw. *Archaeopteryx*, the first bird, is really a dinosaur with feathers. It has a long bony tail, three fingers on its hand, a long thin neck, and a lightly built skull with teeth in its jaws. Modern birds have lost their teeth and their bony tails. The tail is now just a short stump of bones which support the tail feathers. Also, the fingers on the wing have become much smaller, and they do not have claws any longer. Finally, birds today have a breast bone to support the powerful wing muscles.

## PERCHING BIRDS

If the first bird was *Archaeopteryx*, the last, and most successful, birds to evolve were the perching birds. Perching birds evolved about 25 million years ago. About half of all modern birds belong to this group.

Swallows are perching birds.

# EARLY FLYING MACHINES

How could a land-living dinosaur become a flying bird? Did some dinosaurs take to the trees and jump from branch to branch? Or did flying evolve as a way of helping small dinosaurs to leap after insect prey? Indeed, could the early birds like *Archaeopteryx* actually fly, or did they just glide gently from tree to tree? All of these questions are being debated by scientists. Some scientists have even questioned whether *Archaeopteryx* had feathers: they have suggested that the feathers seen in fossils were faked. It seems, however, that the feathers are genuine; they are beautifully preserved in the limestone around the bones. This limestone is so unusual that many other soft-bodied fossils have been found in it, including worms, fish, and other animals.

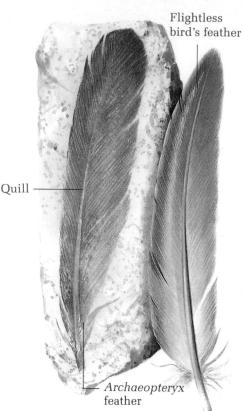

Flightless bird's feather

Quill

*Archaeopteryx* feather

▲ In flying birds, the quill is set to one side. In flightless birds, the quill runs up the middle. So *Archaeopteryx* was a flyer.

▲ One theory about how birds learned to fly is that they first flew **from the ground up**. The prebird dinosaurs may have used their feathered arms to help them leap in the air when catching insects.

▶ Another theory, is that flying began **from the trees down**. Prebird dinosaurs would glide down from trees to catch insects. Over time, the prebirds would have glided farther, until they became fully flying birds.

Hoatzin chick

### A THROWBACK

Do any living birds give clues about the first birds? Baby hoatzins have tiny claws on their wings. They live near rivers in northern South America. Their claws are a throwback to the first birds. The claws don't appear in adult hoatzins.

# DINOFACTS

*Deinonychus*

*Tyrannosaurus*

**Q**: Why did *Deinonychus* die out?

**A**: No one knows. Probably *Deinonychus* lived for five or ten million years, near the end of early Cretaceous times, and then died out. This was long before the famous mass extinction of the dinosaurs, which happened 40 million years later. Possibly, *Deinonychus* disappeared because the animals it fed on, such as *Tenontosaurus*, died out. Or perhaps local climates, in what is now Montana, changed in some way so that this dinosaur could no longer survive.

**Q**: Was *Deinonychus* the most dangerous dinosaur that ever lived?

**A**: *Deinonychus* was the most dangerous small dinosaur. It was shorter than an adult human being, but it could run faster. It would have been able to kill even the strongest man with its terrifying claw. There were other, bigger, meat eaters though. *Tyrannosaurus* was the biggest of all. Forty feet (12 m) long and 20 feet (6 m) high: its mouth opened so wide that a child could have stood up inside (before being swallowed)!

**Q**: What noises did *Deinonychus* make?

**A**: Modern reptiles, such as snakes, can hiss. However, living reptiles cannot sing, since they do not have voice boxes in their throats. Maybe, though, *Deinonychus* was able to sing like its close relatives, the birds. No one knows whether the first birds could sing. But if they could, possibly *Deinonychus* could sing as well. The songs would have been pretty terrible though; screeches and squawks like a rusty old bicycle.

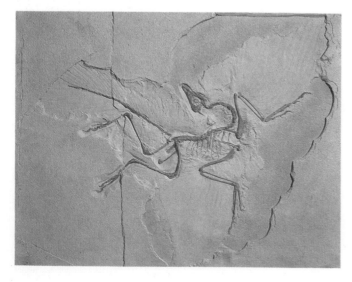

A fossil of *Archaeopteryx*, the first bird

Newly hatched *Deinonychus* young

**Q:** Will scientists ever make a living *Velociraptor*, as is shown in the film *Jurassic Park*?

*Velociraptor*

**Q:** How did *Deinonychus* breed, and what were its babies like?

**A:** So far nobody has found either the eggs or babies of *Deinonychus*. However, all dinosaurs laid eggs, just as birds and most reptiles do today. Probably the eggs were laid in an earth nest on the ground, and then covered with leaves to keep them warm. The babies were probably very small when they hatched. They would have been fierce little monsters that would have snapped and torn at your fingers. The parents would have fed them with lizards and insects, until they were big enough to hunt for themselves.

**Q:** Did *Deinonychus* have any large relatives?

**A:** *Deinonychus* and *Velociraptor* were about the height of eight- or ten-year-old children. But a bigger relative, called informally "*Utahraptor*," has been reported. It is based on a single, sicklelike slashing claw, found in Utah in 1993. So far, all we know is that the claw came from the foot of a dinosaur belonging to the same group as *Deinonychus* (the dromaeosaurs), and that the rocks it was found in were of an earlier period than the Cretaceous.

**A:** Scientists will not be able to build a whole dinosaur for a long time, if ever. The basis of the film is factual: dinosaur cells have been studied for a long time. Recently, dinosaur proteins have been purified in the laboratory. Also, there are many examples of insects that lived in the "Age of the Dinosaurs" that have been preserved in amber (fossil resin), and many of their proteins are still there. The problem is to take these bits of protein and clone them (make them grow) in some way that would ever give you a single cell, let alone a complete living breathing animal. However, who knows what might happen in 50 years time!

Prehistoric insects trapped in amber

# FINDING *DEINONYCHUS*

*Deinonychus* was one of the most exciting recent dinosaur discoveries. In 1964, Professor John Ostrom, and his assistant, Grant Meyer, were out prospecting for dinosaur bones in the Montana Badlands. In the side of a great rounded butte, the two paleontologists spotted some human-sized finger bones. They excitedly brushed away the dirt, and found an extraordinary long three-fingered hand, each finger ending in a fearsome claw. They realized they had found a remarkable new kind of flesh-eating dinosaur.

▲ Professor John Ostrom, pictured shortly after he found *Deinonychus* in 1964.

▶ The first find of *Deinonychus* was two large sharp claws. After careful brushing and scraping away, the rock and dirt were removed to reveal a three-fingered grasping hand.

Ominous Mound, Montana

▼ The *Deinonychus* dig site is located low in a hillside, near the town of Billings, Montana. The 200-foot (60 m)-high butte is made from layers of multicolored sands and muds laid down in ancient rivers and lakes. After Ostrom discovered the foot and hand, he found many more *Deinonychus* bones nearby. It then took him years of careful work in the laboratory before he could reconstruct a skeleton.

— Dig site

▶ *Deinonychus*'s foot was the second part of the skeleton to be found by Ostrom and Meyer. After careful brushing and cleaning, the foot turned out to be complete, and perfectly preserved. The huge claw on the foot gave *Deinonychus* its name of "terrible claw."

# The World of Tyrannosaurus

## Period: Late Cretaceous— 70 million years ago

The king of the tyrant lizards, *Tyrannosaurus* must have filled the world with awe and terror as it pursued its prey some 65 million years ago. Those 5-inch-long teeth, with their sharp edges like serrated steak knives, lined the great tyrannosaur jaws, themselves powered by immense muscles. This fearsome apparatus would have sliced through the thickest of dinosaur skin, readily making a meal of just about anything that came too close.

*Tyrannosaurus* was the largest of meat eaters ever to have lived on land. Up to 40 feet (12m) in length, it was a bipedal (two-legged) form, charging around the landscape on its hind legs. Its long tail was held well above the ground, waggling from side to side to keep the front end of the animal counterbalanced as it walked or ran. And run it must have, if only to ambush or even chase its next meal. These are clues that come from its hideous teeth and claws, and its strong skeletal build.

But not everything is so obvious about the ways of life for a *Tyrannosaurus*. Despite having very long and powerful hind legs, the arms were exceedingly small, barely able to touch one another, let alone help out with the cutting and slicing. They couldn't even reach its powerhouse of a mouth! Though scientists have known that *Tyrannosaurus* had tiny arms for nearly a century, they still don't know exactly why. Perhaps to help *Tyrannosaurus* rear up from a rest? Or for scratching its stomach? Or perhaps to somehow compensate for having such a large head?

Another puzzler is how such a large, predatory animal, with its massive legs, small arms, and long tail, could be related to the robins, pigeons, and ostriches of today. Yet it is true. While not brothers and sisters, or fathers and mothers to birds, meat-eating dinosaurs, including *Tyrannosaurus* and *Deinonychus*, can be considered the closest of cousins in the genealogy of our feathered fliers. How we are confident that this is true—as well as other facts and fancies about its life and times—is revealed here in this comprehensive overview of *Tyrannosaurus*.

**David B. Weishampel**
*Associate Professor*
Johns Hopkins University

# TYRANNOSAURUS TIMELINE

The late Cretaceous, which ended about 65 million years ago, produced many new dinosaur species, among them the giant theropod *Tyrannosaurus*. The dinosaurs of the Jurassic had given way to other groups. The sauropods were now rare, and the most common plant eaters were the hadrosaurs like *Edmontosaurus*. Dinosaurs such as *Triceratops* and *Ankylosaurus* evolved spectacular defensive armor and weaponry. Pachycephalosaurs like *Stegoceras*, and ornithomimids such as *Gallimimus*, appeared for the first time.

*Tyrannosaurus*

*Triceratops*

*Champsosaurus*

► The Cretaceous was the last period of the Mesozoic era, or "Age of Dinosaurs." It lasted from about 145 million to 65 million years ago. At the end of the Cretaceous, the long reign of the giant dinosaurs as rulers of the Earth came to a mysterious end.

*Leptoceratops*

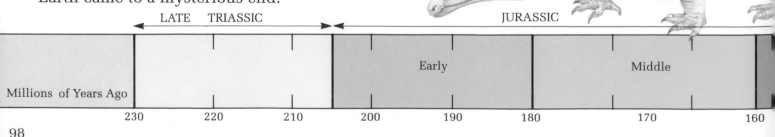

LATE    TRIASSIC    JURASSIC

| | | | Early | | Middle | |
|---|---|---|---|---|---|---|
| Millions of Years Ago | | | | | | |
| 230 | 220 | 210 | 200 | 190 | 180 | 170 | 160 |

▼ The late Cretaceous dinosaur faunas were dominated by herds of the duckbilled hadrosaurs, such as *Edmontosaurus*. *Tyrannosaurus* probably hunted these animals, while its cousin *Ornithomimus* searched for smaller game. Horned dinosaurs ranged from the small *Leptoceratops* to the huge *Triceratops*. Armored dinosaurs such as *Ankylosaurus* were relatively rare. The crocodilelike *Champsosaurus* was not a dinosaur but lived in nearby rivers.

*Edmontosaurus*

*rnithomimus*

*Ankylosaurus*

CRETACEOUS

| | Early | | | | | Late | | | |
|---|---|---|---|---|---|---|---|---|---|
| 145 | 130 | 120 | 110 | 100 | 95 | 90 | 80 | 70 | 65 |

# 70 MILLION YEARS AGO

By the late Cretaceous, the world's continents were nearly in their present positions, but western North America was connected to Asia. Warm seas covered many lands that are now dry. North America was divided by a shallow sea, stretching from the Arctic Ocean to the Gulf of Mexico. Rivers ran from the rising mountains into the sea. In the nearby woodlands lurked *Tyrannosaurus*.

▼ The climate was moderate over most of the world. It was warm in the Arctic. Great herds of duckbills migrated from the dark polar winters, returning north again in the summers.

1. *Triceratops*

2. *Leptoceratops*

3. *Ankylosaurus*

4. *Champsosaurus*

5. *Ornithomimus*

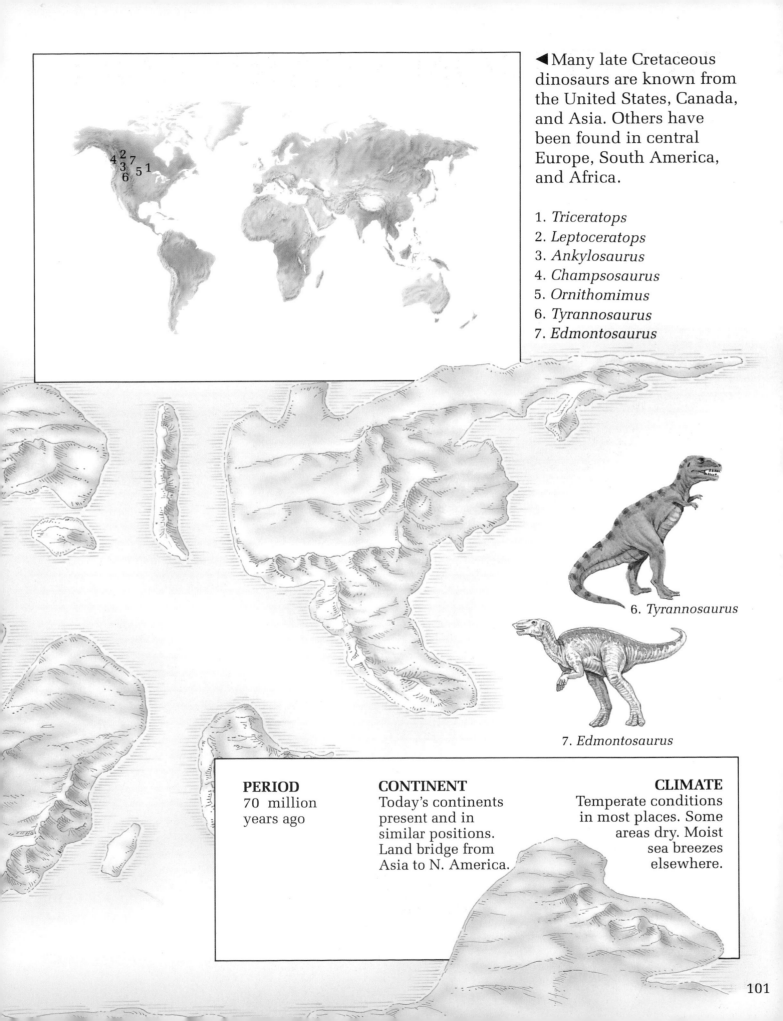

◀ Many late Cretaceous dinosaurs are known from the United States, Canada, and Asia. Others have been found in central Europe, South America, and Africa.

1. *Triceratops*
2. *Leptoceratops*
3. *Ankylosaurus*
4. *Champsosaurus*
5. *Ornithomimus*
6. *Tyrannosaurus*
7. *Edmontosaurus*

6. *Tyrannosaurus*

7. *Edmontosaurus*

**PERIOD**
70 million
years ago

**CONTINENT**
Today's continents
present and in
similar positions.
Land bridge from
Asia to N. America.

**CLIMATE**
Temperate conditions
in most places. Some
areas dry. Moist
sea breezes
elsewhere.

101

# DELTA DAWN

*Tyrannosaurus* was first discovered in late Cretaceous rocks of Montana. These rocks, the Hell Creek Formation, represent ancient rivers and streams, and the large deltas that they built out into the sea. Tall evergreen trees and flowering shrubs grew in the sandy flats of the deltas. Sea breezes cooled the warm night air.

▼ Great dinosaur herds roamed the plains between broad rivers. Some of these were duckbill herds, others horned dinosaur herds.

◄ Great flying reptiles may have scavenged on the bodies of dead dinosaurs, like vultures. This is the cycle of life and death.

▼ The tall conifer tree forests of the late Cretaceous deltas were home to many animals. The trees provided their food and shelter.

▼ Volcanic mountains began to grow in the region where the Rocky Mountains now stand.

◄ *Tyrannosaurus*, the giant hunter, lurked among the shadows of the trees, searching for living or dead prey.

▲ Many modern trees had now evolved. Early sycamores, poplars, and dogwoods left their leaves as fossil imprints in the rocks.

▲ Ankylosaurs, such as *Ankylosaurus*, developed heavy armor for protection from giant theropods. The ankylosaurs were cousins of the Jurassic stegosaurs.

# ANIMALS OF HELL CREEK

Today, Hell Creek, Montana, is a desert with sage brush and scorpions. Seventy million years ago, it was wet and forested, and full of life. This was the end of the "Age of Dinosaurs," when dinosaurs ruled the Earth. Other animals shared this world, however, some of which would be familiar to us today, others that would seem quite strange. Pterosaurs became giants of the air, while the early mammals were small and secretive. Birds and fish were plentiful. Many of the animal groups that live today had not yet evolved, but the plants of the late Cretaceous were very much like the plants that exist today.

## Pterosaurs

The giant pterosaur *Quetzalcoatlus* was a flying reptile, the size of a small airplane.

## Plants

Flowering plants were part of the Cretaceous scene. Magnolias, dogwoods, and colorful shrubs attracted the attention of nectar-seeking insects.

## Mammals

Marsupials, like *Alphadon*, reared their babies in pouches. Insect eaters, such as *Gypsonictops*, were shrewlike.

*Alphadon*        *Gypsonictops*

## Birds

Modern-style birds were already present in the late Cretaceous. *Tytthostonyx* was similar to modern seagulls.

## Fish

*Enchodus* was a bony fish with very large teeth. It swam alongside *Lepisosteus*, a species closely related to the modern garfish. On the bottom of the sandy rivers lived the saw-toothed skate, *Sclerorhynchus*.

*Enchodus*

*Lepisosteus*

*Sclerorhynchus*

## Crocodiles

The rivers were full of crocodiles. *Deinosuchus* was 40 feet (12 m) long, and probably ate small dinosaurs if they got too close to the water's edge!

# PEACEFUL NEIGHBORS

The giant theropod, *Tyrannosaurus*, lived in a world full of dinosaurs, many of them plant eaters living in fear of hungry tyrannosaurs. Paleontologists are piecing together the lives of these dinosaurs. Most dinosaurs were not slow and stupid, but active agile creatures. Some probably had structured family lives and complex behavior. The hadrosaurs, or duckbills, for instance, apparently lived in great herds and looked after their young while they were in the nest. Pachycephalosaurs may have competed with rivals for the attention of a mate. They seem to have butted their thick-skulled heads together, in the same way that rams do today.

*Edmontosaurus*

ed-MONT-oh-SAW-rus
"EDMONTON REPTILE"
42 FT. 6 IN. (13 M) LONG

A very common duckbilled hadrosaur.

Nest

Young *Edmontosaurus*

Eggs

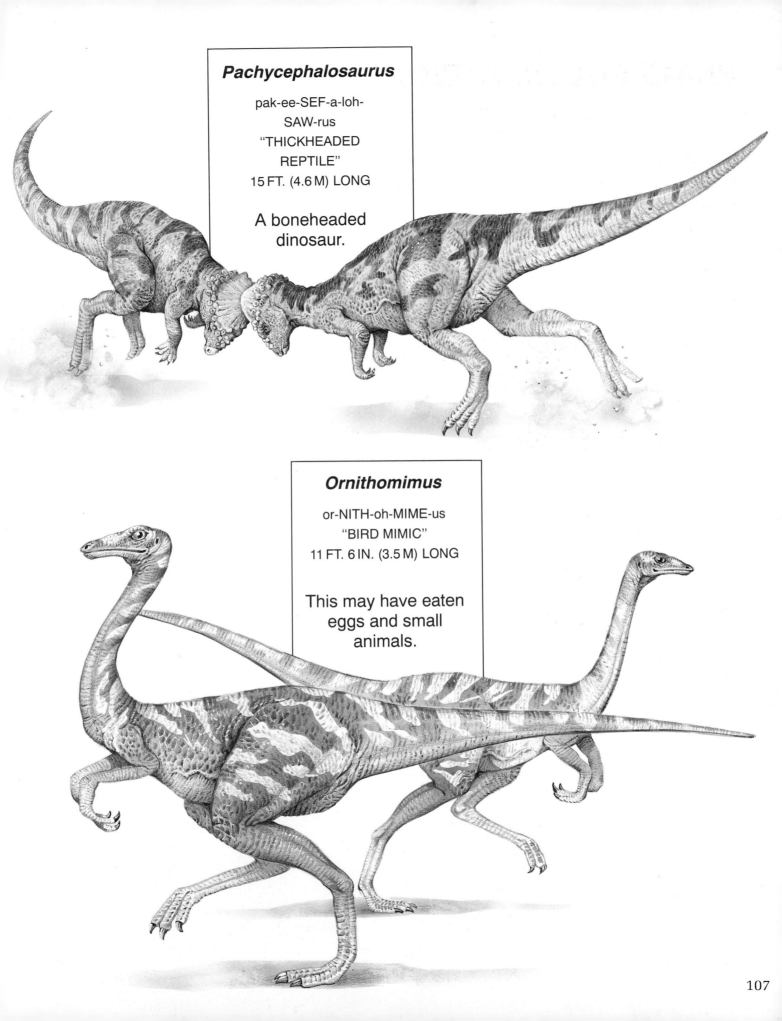

### Pachycephalosaurus

pak-ee-SEF-a-loh-
SAW-rus
"THICKHEADED
REPTILE"
15 FT. (4.6 M) LONG

A boneheaded
dinosaur.

### Ornithomimus

or-NITH-oh-MIME-us
"BIRD MIMIC"
11 FT. 6 IN. (3.5 M) LONG

This may have eaten
eggs and small
animals.

# DIFFICULT DINNERS

*Tyrannosaurus* was a carnivorous (meat-eating) theropod and killed other dinosaurs for food. It is the largest known carnivore, and must have been a fearsome enemy. Many late Cretaceous dinosaurs, however, were well equipped to withstand the attacks of *Tyrannosaurus*. Some, like the ankylosaurs and their cousins the nodosaurs, had heavy armor for protection. Others had weapons of their own, such as clubs and horns, that could injure, cripple, or perhaps kill a hungry attacker. The horned ceratopsians had the most obvious defensive weaponry. No wonder that *Tyrannosaurus* probably preferred easier game.

*Euoplocephalus*

yu-OP-lo-SEF-a-lus
"WELL-ARMORED HEAD"
23 FT. (7 M) LONG

Many ankylosaurs had a heavy bony club at the end of the tail. A blow from this club could cripple a giant predator.

*Panoplosaurus*

pan-OH-plo-SAW-rus
"FULLY-ARMORED REPTILE"
23 FT. (7 M) LONG

This armored nodosaur was well protected from enemies.

## Triceratops

try-SAIR-a-tops
"THREE-HORNED FACE"
30 FT. (9 M) LONG

The horned dinosaurs were unique to the Cretaceous and were formidable adversaries. With its three great horns, *Triceratops* might counter *Tyrannosaurus* with a direct charge.

# KING OF THE CRETACEOUS

*Tyrannosaurus* means "tyrant reptile," and it must certainly have been the lord of all it surveyed. It was the last and largest "carnosaur," or giant carnivorous dinosaur, growing up to 40 feet (12 m) long, and it had no natural enemies. This spectacular animal, in spite of its tremendous size and huge toothed jaws, had hollow bones, three prominent toes, and a bipedal (two-legged) stance —all characteristics shared with its smaller cousins the birds! It has even been suggested that it was warm-blooded, like birds, but we may never know if this was true because only *Tyrannosaurus* bones and teeth have been preserved.

▼ Few intact skeletons of *Tyrannosaurus* have been found. Nevertheless, they give us a complete picture of this dinosaur's appearance.

Tail vertebrae

▼ We now know that *Tyrannosaurus* balanced its body horizontally, with its tail held out behind. The head was on an S-shaped neck, like that of a bird.

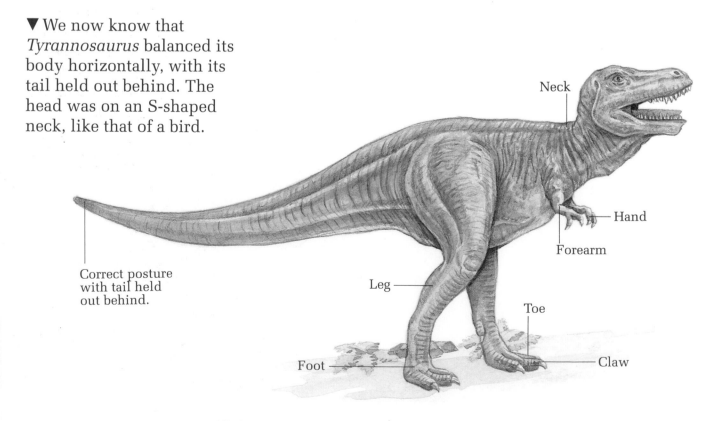

Neck

Hand

Forearm

Leg

Correct posture with tail held out behind.

Toe

Foot

Claw

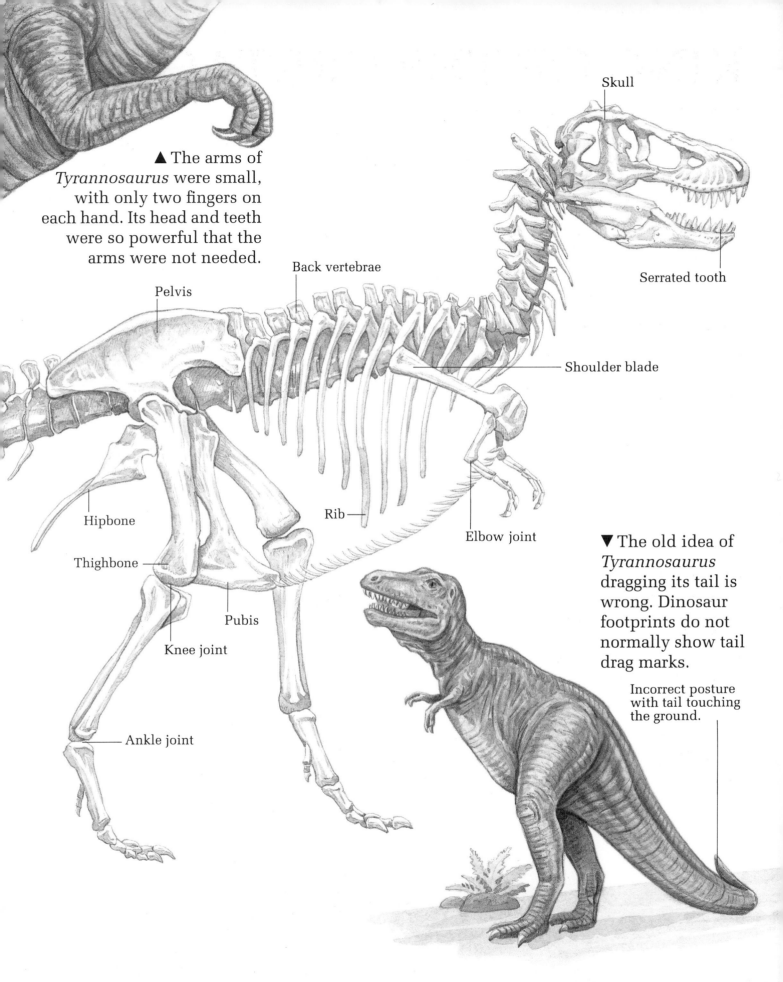

▲ The arms of *Tyrannosaurus* were small, with only two fingers on each hand. Its head and teeth were so powerful that the arms were not needed.

Skull

Serrated tooth

Back vertebrae

Pelvis

Shoulder blade

Hipbone

Rib

Elbow joint

Thighbone

Pubis

▼ The old idea of *Tyrannosaurus* dragging its tail is wrong. Dinosaur footprints do not normally show tail drag marks.

Knee joint

Incorrect posture with tail touching the ground.

Ankle joint

# MAKING A LIVING

It is clear from its teeth that *Tyrannosaurus* ate meat, but did it actually hunt and kill its own food? Some people have suggested that it only fed off the carcasses of animals that were already dead, perhaps because it was too big and slow to chase other dinosaurs. In fact, *Tyrannosaurus*'s strong jaw muscles, long sharp teeth, powerful legs, large claws, and relatively big brain show that it was surely able to kill for itself. *Tyrannosaurus* was certainly a successful predator. Perhaps it did not need to be terribly fast, for it may have ambushed unsuspecting dinosaurs by springing out from a concealed position—although such a big dinosaur would be hard to hide!

▼ The feet of *Tyrannosaurus* were perfectly made for supporting its bulky body. The splayed toes and large claws spread the animal's weight.

Toe

Claw

*Corythosaurus*

kor-ITH-oh-SAW-rus
"HELMETED REPTILE"
33 FT. (10 M) LONG

A lambeosaurine duckbill.

## TOOLS OF THE TRADE

The massive head of *Tyrannosaurus* had a wide and gaping mouth, full of steak-knife teeth. It could cut out and swallow huge chunks of meat without chewing. The teeth were up to 6 inches (15 cm) long, and had sharp cutting edges, with sawlike serrations. These teeth were constantly replaced, as old teeth wore down and fell out.

A *Tyrannosaurus* tooth

▼ *Tyrannosaurus* could certainly scavenge its food. Such a large dinosaur could easily have taken food from other animals. The smell of a fresh kill might have attracted tyrannosaurs from far and wide.

113

# RUNNING THE RACE

How did *Tyrannosaurus* move? Was it big and slow, or did it run quickly? Its bones give us some clues. The proportions of its limbs suggest that it was a quick, agile animal, but not one with great speed. Its broad, birdlike feet provided good balance, but its long thigh bone shows that it could not move its legs very rapidly. Probably, *Tyrannosaurus* could chase its prey, but only catch the weakest and slowest animals. Certainly, *Tyrannosaurus* did not have to run *away* from anything!

◀ The old idea of *Tyrannosaurus* as an ungainly, lumbering monster—slow and clumsy, and unable to catch its own food—is certainly wrong. It was built to hunt.

▼ *Tyrannosaurus* was probably very birdlike in its movements. It could run, but was certainly not very fast—not as fast as a horse, for example.

Footprints of a large, three-toed dinosaur

▼ Fossil footprints of dinosaurs give the paleontologist an idea of their movement and behavior. Measuring the gaps between them gives an estimate of speed, once we know the dinosaur's approximate height.

# NEXT MEAL

When *Tyrannosaurus* was on the prowl, there was no lack of other dinosaurs to eat, but not all were easy to kill. Because so many late Cretaceous dinosaurs had evolved strong defenses against predators, *Tyrannosaurus* probably often ate duck-billed hadrosaurs. They were plentiful, and had no horns or bony armor for protection. Perhaps the duckbills formed the biggest part, if not all, of a tyrannosaur's diet. All hadrosaurs were herbivores (plant eaters).

▼ Without natural defenses of its own, the hadrosaur's back was vulnerable to the bite of a tyrannosaur. We often find tyrannosaur teeth in hadrosaur bones.

► One of the most common Cretaceous dinosaurs was *Edmontosaurus*. Like other hadrosaurs, it had a broad duck-like bill, with which it cropped conifer needles and other plant food.

African lions chasing
an antelope.

▶ Hadrosaurs probably
lived in herds for
safety, just like
antelopes do today.
*Tyrannosaurus* would
have killed the weakest
animals, much in the
way that lions pick out
the easiest prey.

## A FOOD PROCESSOR

▶ Duckbills had hundreds of
small, blunt teeth for grinding
up plants. Unlike today's
reptiles, hadrosaurs could
chew their food.

Horny beak

Teeth at
back of mouth

Hooflike
toenails

◀ The toes of hadrosaurs were
broad and hooflike. They
were good for walking over
marshy ground, but were no
match for the claws of a
tyrannosaur.

# THE TYRANNOSAUR FAMILY

*Tyrannosaurus* was one of several similar dinosaurs, although it was the largest tyrannosaur, and is the most famous. Tyrannosaurs are so far known only from the late Cretaceous period of North America and Asia. They were the last in a long line of giant meat eaters, which began in the Triassic age with small forms like *Coelophysis*, and included *Allosaurus* from the Jurassic. The tyrannosaur family mysteriously became extinct with all other large dinosaurs (leaving only avian theropods— the birds) at the end of the Cretaceous period.

## Nanotyrannus

NAN-oh-tie-RAN-us
"DWARF TYRANT"
16 FT. (5 M) LONG

This recently discovered tyrannosaur is from Montana.

## Tyrannosaurus

tie-RAN-oh-SAW-rus
"TYRANT REPTILE"
40 FT. (12 M) LONG

The most famous tyrannosaur was also the largest.

## Tarbosaurus

TARB-oh-SAW-rus
"ALARMING REPTILE"
33 FT. (10 M) LONG

A smaller cousin of *Tyrannosaurus*, from Mongolia in Asia.

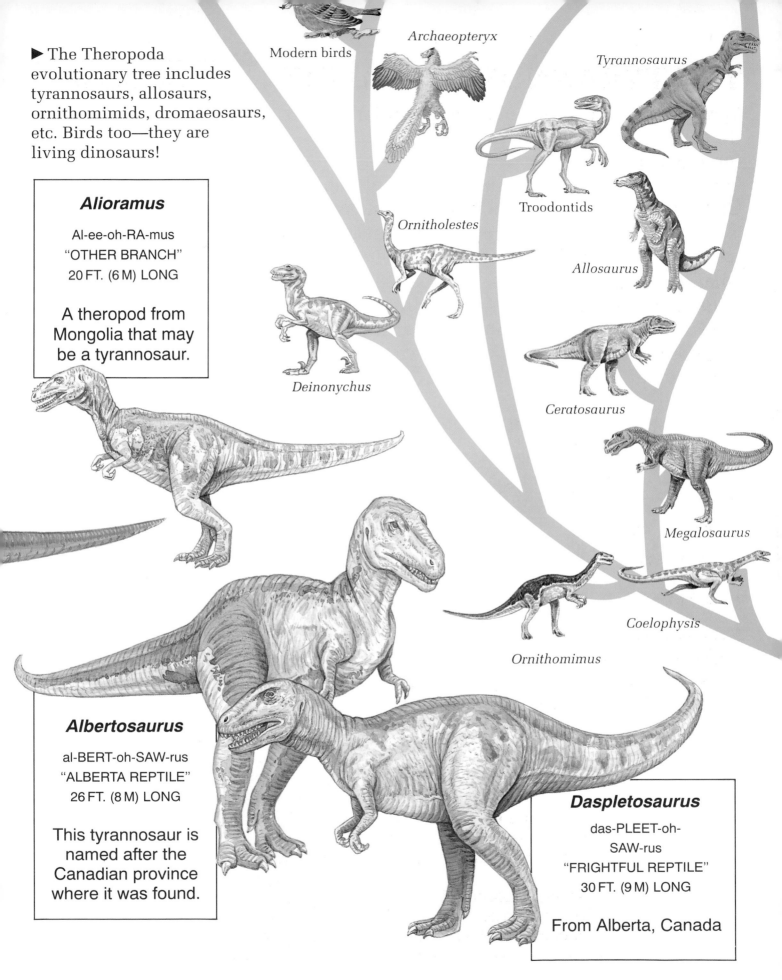

▶ The Theropoda evolutionary tree includes tyrannosaurs, allosaurs, ornithomimids, dromaeosaurs, etc. Birds too—they are living dinosaurs!

Modern birds

*Archaeopteryx*

Tyrannosaurus

Troodontids

*Ornitholestes*

Allosaurus

### *Alioramus*

Al-ee-oh-RA-mus
"OTHER BRANCH"
20 FT. (6 M) LONG

A theropod from Mongolia that may be a tyrannosaur.

*Deinonychus*

*Ceratosaurus*

*Megalosaurus*

*Coelophysis*

*Ornithomimus*

### *Albertosaurus*

al-BERT-oh-SAW-rus
"ALBERTA REPTILE"
26 FT. (8 M) LONG

This tyrannosaur is named after the Canadian province where it was found.

### *Daspletosaurus*

das-PLEET-oh-SAW-rus
"FRIGHTFUL REPTILE"
30 FT. (9 M) LONG

From Alberta, Canada

# TOWARD EXTINCTION

All the giant dinosaurs became extinct at or near the end of the late Cretaceous period, about 65 million years ago. No one knows why, although there have been many theories. Some of the old ideas are outrageously fanciful. For instance, it has been suggested that the dinosaurs were killed by poisonous air, a lack of minerals, cosmic radiation, floods, sunspots, volcanoes, overeating, or over population. It was even said that dinosaurs were too stupid to survive—even though they existed for over 150 million years! When we talk about why the dinosaurs became extinct, it's worth noting that human beings have only been around for about two million years.

▼ A once popular idea was that drought, starvation, and disease killed the dinosaurs. The climate and environment of the world are always changing, but did they change so suddenly that dinosaurs could not cope?

▼ A silly notion to explain the extinction is that the food supply became poisonous. Although many plants have toxins for defense against herbivores, dinosaurs would have avoided inedible plants.

◀ *Parasaurolophus*, was a very successful plant eater. There is no evidence at all to think that it was killed by its food!

▶ Did small mammals eat too many of the dinosaurs' eggs? No baby dinosaurs would mean eventual extinction. This is obviously incorrect, because the dinosaurs and early mammals coexisted for millions of years.

# DINOFACTS

**Q:** How can you tell the difference between a male and female *Tyrannosaurus*?

▼ We can tell the difference between a female and male mallard duck by their different-colored plumage.

Female mallard

Male mallard

**A:** This is very hard to do from fossils. Maybe a very large *Tyrannosaurus* skeleton would be that of a male, while the female was smaller, or vice versa. In many modern reptiles and birds the female is often larger than her mate. Also, the sexes of some animals today, especially birds, are different colors. Perhaps the color of *Tyrannosaurus* was different in males and females. A new theory suggests that the bones at the base of the tail were different to allow for the passage of eggs.

**Q:** Has a complete *Tyrannosaurus* fossil ever been found?

**A:** A new *Tyrannosaurus* skeleton was recently discovered in Montana. It is one of the most complete and biggest examples ever found of this dinosaur. It is now being studied by scientists at the Museum of the Rockies, at Bozeman, Montana. Yet another new *Tyrannosaurus* from South Dakota, is now the object of an ownership dispute in the courts. Unfortunately, fossils have become big business.

**Q:** How big was *Tyrannosaurus*?

**A:** This would depend on the age and sex of an individual. Just as in animals today, dinosaurs came in a variety of sizes. Naturally, the young animals would have been smaller than adults. Also, male dinosaurs may have been larger than the females, or vice versa. Of course, even two adults might be different in size. The largest *Tyrannosaurus* was probably about 40 feet (12 m) long.

**Q:** How much did *Tyrannosaurus* weigh?

**A:** We can estimate the weight of a dinosaur from its size while alive. Because animals are made up mostly of water, they weigh only a little less than the same amount of water. If we make a lifelike model of a dinosaur, we will know the amount of water it equals, by the amount it will displace in a measured container. It is then easy to scale the estimate up to full size. Because an adult *Tyrannosaurus* was so big, it may have weighed 5 or 6 tons.

▲ Complete dinosaur skeletons are very rare, so a new *Tyrannosaurus* will give us lots of new information.

**Q:** Why was *Tyrannosaurus* so vicious?

**A:** It is wrong to say that this was a vicious animal. It made its living by being a hunter and was only good at its job! Various organisms obtain food in many different ways. Some animals, such as *Tyrannosaurus*, eat meat, and they must be good hunters to survive. *Tyrannosaurus* had very efficient hunting tools in its teeth and certainly must have seemed ferocious, but it did not kill out of spite.

▼ This *Edmontosaurus* died of natural causes, but some skeletons contain theropod teeth, showing they were eaten.

**Q:** When was the last *Tyrannosaurus* alive?

**A:** The last one died at the close of the Cretaceous period. It is still a mystery why such dinosaurs disappeared. If, as some scientists think, they were killed by an asteroid or comet hitting the Earth, *Tyrannosaurus* was just unlucky.

► The meteor crater at Wolf Creek, Australia, is one of the largest in the world. It shows the tremendous power potential of extra-terrestrial objects.

# FINDING *TYRANNOSAURU*

The first *Tyrannosaurus* was discovered in 1902, by Barnum Brown of the American Museum of Natural History. He traveled from New York to prospect for dinosaurs in Montana. His boss was the celebrated paleontologist Henry F. Osborn, who described the new fossil skeleton, and gave it the famous name everyone knows today. Montana is a particularly good place to find dinosaur fossils, because many of the rocks there are of the right age, are river and delta sediments where dinosaurs lived, and are well exposed in desert "badlands."

▶ A *Tyrannosaurus* skeleton, erected at the museum, has fascinated generations of schoolchildren. It even inspired some of them to become paleontologists!

◀ Barnum Brown (hammer in hand) collects a dinosaur leg bone with H. F. Osborn. You can see that the landscape (at Como Bluff) is dry and barren.

▼ Traditional methods of collecting dinosaurs relied on horses, wagons, and manual labor. Today, we use off-road vehicles, jackhammers, and much more—sometimes even helicopters. Brute force and hard work, however, will never be obsolete!

# Dinoworld Questions and Answers

**S**o you think you're an expert on the world of the dinosaurs? Now you can test your knowledge with Dinoworld Questions and Answers!

Which were the deadliest dinosaurs?

Could dinosaurs fly?

Which were the fastest dinosaurs?

Which dinosaurs had back plates?

What happened to the dinosaurs?

What came after the dinosaurs?

Were all dinosaurs huge?

127

# How do we know about ancient life?

Clues about ancient life are hidden in the Earth's crust. Most rocks are made up of layers of mud and sand, rather like a giant sandwich. Over millions of years, the layers were squeezed and cemented together, eventually becoming hard. The bones and shells of animals trapped in the layers also turned to stone, forming fossils. Scientists learn about ancient life by studying fossils and the rocks in which they are found.

2 The position of each bone is recorded, to help scientists piece the animal back together later on.

1 The fossilized bones of ancient animals can easily be damaged. Great care is taken when uncovering them.

**3** Photographs are also taken, both of the way the fossilized skeleton is lying, and of the rock and soil layers.

 **DISCOVERY FACTS**

● In 1810, 12-year-old Mary Anning and her brother Joseph became the first people to find the fossilized skeleton of a sea reptile, later named an ichthyosaur (see page 31).

**4** Each fossilized bone is encased in a layer of plaster of Paris. This protects it on its way to the museum.

 **HOW FOSSILS FORM**

**1** The dead body of an animal sinks to the bottom of a lake, river, or sea.

**2** Its skeleton is buried by layers of sand and mud. Millions of years now pass.

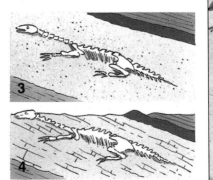

**3** The sand and mud turn to rock. The bones become fossils.

**4** In time, the rocks wear away and the fossil appears at the surface.

# When did life begin?

The Earth is so old that most of its history is a mystery to us. However, scientists believe that the Earth began about 4.6 billion years ago, and that life first appeared about a billion years later.

The oldest fossils ever found date back to 600 million years ago. It wasn't until then that animals developed the hard shells and bones that could form fossils. The soft bodies of earlier animals just rotted away.

With their long stalks, crinoids looked like plants. They were really animals, the relatives of today's starfish.

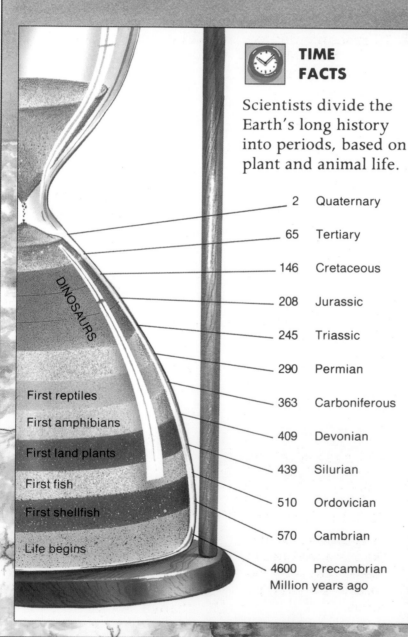

### TIME FACTS

Scientists divide the Earth's long history into periods, based on plant and animal life.

| | |
|---|---|
| 2 | Quaternary |
| 65 | Tertiary |
| 146 | Cretaceous |
| 208 | Jurassic |
| 245 | Triassic |
| 290 | Permian |
| 363 | Carboniferous |
| 409 | Devonian |
| 439 | Silurian |
| 510 | Ordovician |
| 570 | Cambrian |
| 4600 | Precambrian |

Million years ago

DINOSAURS

First reptiles

First amphibians

First land plants

First fish

First shellfish

Life begins

Calcichordates were related to crinoids. They crawled along the seabed, pushing with their tails.

Some of the oldest fossils ever found are of the coiled shells of sea snails rather like the whelks of today.

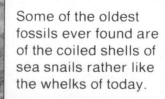

The Silurian seas must have been full of the animals we call graptolites. Their fossils are quite common.

All Silurian animals lived in the sea. Trilobites prowled for food on the seabed. They were rather like early crabs.

Early corals looked like sea anemones in shells. They were the ancestors of today's corals.

## EVOLVE AN ANIMAL

There are two main groups of animal today —those with backbones and those without. Backboned animals didn't develop until Silurian times. Here's how to trace what happened:

**1** Make a tadpole-like creature out of modeling clay.

**2** To help it to swim, squeeze its tail into a fin. Your animal will still be very floppy.

**3** Stiffen it by pushing in a pencil backbone.

Living things develop and change very, very slowly, over millions of years. We call this long, slow process of change "evolution."

# What were the first fish like?

The first fish looked rather like tadpoles—
*Arandaspis* (below) had a head, a backbone,
and a tail, but no fins. Fish evolved in the
Ordovician period. They were the first
animals to have proper backbones.

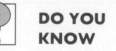 **DO YOU KNOW**

None of the first fish
had jaws. Although
*Drebanaspis* and
*Hemicyclaspis* evolved
after *Arandaspis*, they
also sucked in food
instead of biting it.

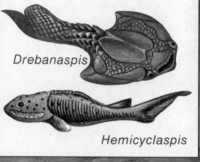

Drebanaspis

Hemicyclaspis

# Which fish was as big as a whale?

*Dunkleosteus* was an amazing 32 feet long.
It had armorlike skin and its huge jaws were
filled with razor-sharp cutters. It must have
been the terror of the ancient seas.

 **DO YOU KNOW**

Predators are animals
that hunt and eat other
animals. They are fast
movers, with good
eyes and sharp beaks
or teeth—like sharks
and crocodiles today.

# How old are sharks?

Sharks form one of the oldest animal groups alive today. Their ancestors developed 400 million years ago, in the Devonian seas.

*Stethacanthus* (below) was a very odd-looking shark that lived about 300 million years ago.

**DO YOU KNOW**

*Cladoselache* was one of the first sharks, evolving even before *Stethacanthus*.

*Xenacanthus* also appeared in Devonian times, but it outlived the other two types.

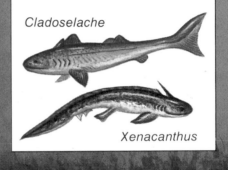

Cladoselache

Xenacanthus

# Which fish could breathe out of water?

At the same time as sharks were evolving, other fish, called lungfish, were developing a way of breathing air and living on dry land. They were probably tempted ashore by the insects that were now living there.

*Panderichthys* was an early land-going lungfish. To help them move on land, these fish developed sturdy fleshy fins.

As well as gills for breathing in water, lungfish had lungs for breathing in air.

# Which were the first landlubbers?

Lungfish were only able to live on land for short periods of time. Gradually, however, new animals evolved which could spend most of their lives out of water—the amphibians. Amphibians could breathe air and, as they spent more and more time on land, their fleshy fins slowly evolved into strong legs. They couldn't live far from water, though, or their slimy skins dried out. They laid their eggs in water, too.

**DO YOU KNOW**

*Ichthyostega* was an early amphibian. Like its fish ancestors, it had a fish's head and a tail with a fin. But it had legs instead of fleshy fins, and feet with toes, showing that it lived mostly on land.

*Eryops* was the size of a pig. Its thick skin was like armor, and helped to support its body weight on land.

*Eogyrinus* must have spent a lot of its life in water—its tail was finlike, and its legs were short.

*Eogyrinus* was as long as a car. It lived like a crocodile, chasing fish through the swamp waters.

## AMPHIBIAN FACTS

• The word amphibian means "leading a double life."

• Amphibians spend only part of their lives on land. They must lay their eggs in water and spend the early part of their lives as swimming animals.

• Newts and toads are modern amphibians.

All sorts of different amphibians evolved during the Carboniferous period. The land was covered with forests of treelike ferns at that time.

*Keraterpeton* was a small salamanderlike amphibian with a long tail. It probably ate insects.

*Phlegethonia* had no legs. It burrowed like a worm through the rotting vegetation of the forest floor.

# When were dragonflies as big as birds?

Huge flying insects lived at the same time as the amphibians in the thick Carboniferous forests. Dragonflies the size of birds flew around the forest swamps, and many different kinds of crawling insects thrived in the lush vegetation. Insects were among the first animals to live on dry land, attracted by the new plants growing there.

The damp Carboniferous forests must have been buzzing with the sound of flying insects. The lush plant life provided them with plenty of food.

 **CRAWLER FACTS**

● *Brontoscorpio* (below) was as big as a cat. Like many of the first scorpions, it could live both on land and in the water.

● The giant millipede *Arthropleura* (above) was nearly 6 feet long. It fed on rotting vegetation in the ferny undergrowth.

*Meganeura* was probably the biggest dragonfly ever. It had a wingspan of 27 inches —that's the same as a modern parrot's!

# When did the first reptiles appear?

Reptiles began to evolve about 350 million years ago. They were different from the amphibians in a very important way. Although amphibians are suited to life on land, they always have to return to the water to lay their eggs—these have to stay moist. Reptiles' eggs can be laid on land because they are protected by a leathery shell. Reptiles were the first true land-dwellers.

**REPTILE FACTS**

● The first reptile was *Westlothiana*, a lizard like animal about 4 inches long. It lived among the amphibians in the Carboniferous forests.

*Westlothiana*

*Coelurosauravus* was a gliding reptile about the size of a frisbee.

The slow-moving reptile *Pareiasaurus* was as big as a cow. Its broad mouth was just right for chewing tough plants.

# Where did mammals come from?

Mammals evolved from a group of animals called mammal-like reptiles. These reptiles had differently shaped teeth for killing and chewing. Over millions of years, their legs became straighter, holding the animal clear of the ground. By the end of the Triassic period, they had developed into the mammals themselves.

*Megazostrodon* was one of the first mammals. Like many modern mammals, it had warm fur, and whiskers to help it feel its way about.

Mammals do not lay eggs, but give birth to young animals. The babies feed on their mother's milk.

 **FAMILY FACTS**

*Dimetrodon*

• *Lycaenops* was the size of a small dog. *Massetognathus* was one of the last of the mammal-like reptiles, and among the first to have fur on its body.

• *Dimetrodon* was one of the first mammal-like reptiles. The stiff fin on its back gave off heat and kept the animal cool.

*Lycaenops*

*Massetognathus*

# What were ruling reptiles?

The animal group that we call the ruling reptiles lived at the same time as the mammal-like reptiles. They had strong hind legs and long tails, and looked rather like crocodiles. The animals that evolved from them belonged to three different groups. One group evolved into the crocodiles, another into the pterosaurs (see page 28), and a third into the dinosaurs.

(see page 28)

**DO YOU KNOW**

Today's crocodiles still have the sharp teeth, long tail and strong legs of their distant ancestors, such as *Chasmatosaurus*, one of the first ruling reptiles.

*Chasmatosaurus*

Crocodile

*Ornithosuchus* was one of the later ruling reptiles. It lived on land, and could walk upright on two legs, using its long tail for balance.

*Ornithosuchus* may have gone on two legs only when it ran, spending the rest of the time on all fours.

# When did dinosaurs first appear?

The first dinosaurs evolved from the ruling reptiles about 225 million years ago—toward the middle of the Triassic period. Early dinosaurs were small and rare, but in time they became more common and much larger. The first dinosaurs were mostly two-legged meat eaters, but new kinds slowly evolved, and some of them ate plants. The bodies of plant-eating dinosaurs developed quite differently from those of meat eaters.

Insects and lizards were a tasty meal in the deserts where *Procompsognathus* lived. But it had to catch them first!

*Procompsognathus* was one of the first dinosaurs. About the size of a vulture, it chased its prey on its long hind legs.

### EATING FACTS

● Early dinosaurs were two legged meat eaters like *Procompsognathus*. Four-legged plant eaters like *Plateosaurus* evolved later. Plants are tougher to digest than meat—it takes longer to break them down and get the goodness out.

The conifers eaten by some dinosaurs were very hard to digest.

● In animals, digestion takes place in a long tube off the stomach, called the intestine. Plant-eating dinosaurs evolved longer intestines, and huge bodies to fit them in! Their size meant they had to go on four legs instead of two. Two-legged plant eaters evolved much later.

*Plateosaurus* was one of the first of the large plant-eating dinosaurs. Its long neck helped it to nibble the treetops.

*Plateosaurus* walked on all fours, but could stand on its hind legs to feed. It was about 25 feet long.

## HIP FACTS

● Scientists divide dinosaurs by the shape of their hip bones. There are two main groups—lizard-hipped and bird-hipped. All the meat eaters and the really big four-legged plant eaters were lizard-hipped.

*Albertosaurus* (lizard-hipped meat eater)

*Alamosaurus* (lizard-hipped plant eater)

● The bird-hipped dinosaurs evolved later. They were all plant eaters—both two-legged and four-legged ones.

*Kritosaurus* (bird-hipped)

# Which were the giant dinosaurs?

The long-necked plant eaters that evolved from *Plateosaurus* were the largest land animals of all time. Some were more than ten times the size of an elephant. Known as sauropods, these giants thrived at the end of the Jurassic period, when the lush plant life provided plenty of good food.

Sauropods had big bodies with a long neck and a tiny head. They could reach the treetops to feed on their diet of leaves and twigs. At their size, they must have spent nearly all their time just eating!

*Brachiosaurus* was one of the tallest dinosaurs. It could raise its head 42 feet above ground — that's as high as a four-story building!

 **SIZE FACTS**

● *Mamenchisaurus* had the longest neck ever. At 50 feet, it was longer than four cars parked end to end.

● Sauropod hip bones were huge. One found in Colorado, in 1988, turned out to be bigger than a man.

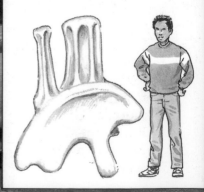

*Apatosaurus* was 70 feet long. Its tail made up nearly half its body length, and may have been lashed like a whip to frighten off attackers.

### DINOSAUR PRINTS

How to make perfect prehistoric prints!

**1** Cut a potato in two and draw a dinosaur shape on each surface —practice this first.

**2** Very carefully, cut round your shape with a knife, so that it is slightly raised.

**3** Coat your dinosaur with paint, and print!

A long neck and tail made *Diplodocus* one of the longest dinosaurs. At 90 feet, it was equal to seven cars parked end to end!

# Were all dinosaurs huge?

We usually think of dinosaurs as huge monsters, the size of houses. In fact, many were quite small. Some were no bigger than today's lizards and songbirds.

These dinosaurs included plant eaters, and meat eaters that fed on insects or on animals even smaller than themselves.

**DO YOU KNOW**

Dinosaur names are Latin. They are often long, and hard to say. Many of them simply describe a dinosaur's appearance. For example, *Styracosaurus* means "spiked reptile."

*Compsognathus* had a thin tail which was more than twice as long as its body.

*Compsognathus* was about the size of a chicken, and fast on its feet. It was a meat eater and fed on small lizards.

**DO YOU KNOW**

*Scutellosaurus* was another tiny dino- saur—it would only have been the size of a cat if it were alive today! Rows of studs protected this plant eater along its back and tail.

# Where was the smallest skeleton found?

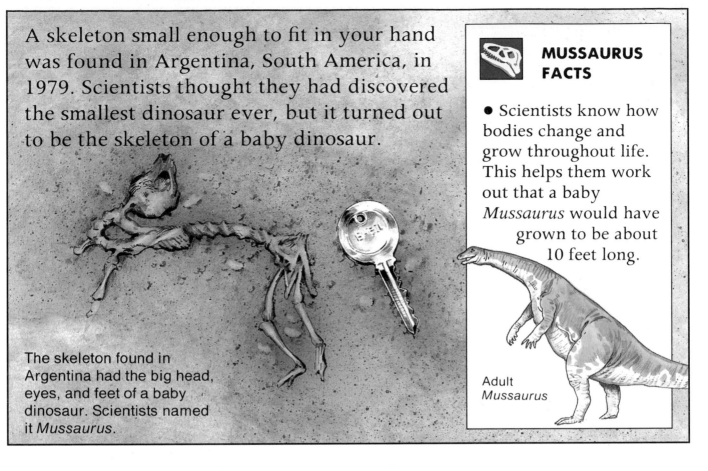

A skeleton small enough to fit in your hand was found in Argentina, South America, in 1979. Scientists thought they had discovered the smallest dinosaur ever, but it turned out to be the skeleton of a baby dinosaur.

The skeleton found in Argentina had the big head, eyes, and feet of a baby dinosaur. Scientists named it *Mussaurus*.

## MUSSAURUS FACTS

● Scientists know how bodies change and grow throughout life. This helps them work out that a baby *Mussaurus* would have grown to be about 10 feet long.

Adult *Mussaurus*

# Where was the smallest footprint found?

A dinosaur footprint no bigger than a modern sparrow's was discovered among rocks in Nova Scotia, Canada, in the 1980s. Reptiles don't live there today, as it's much too cold. The climate must have been warmer 150 million years ago!

A fossilized footprint may be all scientists know about an animal. This type of record is called a trace fossil.

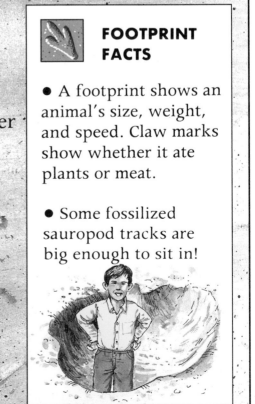

## FOOTPRINT FACTS

● A footprint shows an animal's size, weight, and speed. Claw marks show whether it ate plants or meat.

● Some fossilized sauropod tracks are big enough to sit in!

145

# Which were the fastest dinosaurs?

The meat-eaters were the fastest of all the dinosaurs because of the way their bodies were built. They moved on strong hind legs, balanced by a heavy tail. This allowed them to run very quickly, which helped them to catch their supper! Hunters always have to run faster than their prey—otherwise they simply won't eat enough to survive.

*Troodon* held its long tail out stiffly as it ran, making a perfect balance for its long neck, and helping it run at top speed.

The fierce meat-eating dinosaur *Troodon* was the size of an emu. It could run at speed on its long hind legs.

*Troodon* was a deadly hunter. The huge curved claw on each hind foot was used to slash its prey to death.

## SPEED FACTS

● *Struthiomimus* was one of the fastest dinosaurs. It was about the size and shape of an ostrich, and with its huge stride, it may have run as fast as 30 miles per hour.

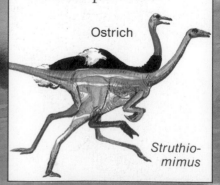

Ostrich

Struthio-mimus

# Which were the deadliest dinosaurs?

The meat-eating dinosaurs weren't just fast—they were the most ferocious animals that have ever lived. As time went on, larger and faster kinds evolved. *Tyrannosaurus* was the biggest of them all, measuring over 40 feet —about the length of three cars! With its powerful legs and razorlike jaws, it must have been a terrifyingly efficient killer.

*Tyrannosaurus*'s head was more than 3 feet long. Its deadly teeth were as big and as jagged as steak knives.

*Tyrannosaurus*'s arms were surprisingly small. Each hand had only two clawed fingers, possibly used for picking its teeth.

*Tyrannosaurus* had strong legs with huge feet. They had to be sturdy enough to carry the dinosaur's great bulk while it attacked.

**MEAT-EATER FACTS**

● *Spinosaurus* lived in Africa. It was as long as *Tyrannosaurus*, but more lightly built.

# Why did some dinosaurs have horns?

Plant-eating dinosaurs needed to protect themselves from fierce meat eaters like *Tyrannosaurus*. Some kinds developed horns to scare off their attackers. *Triceratops* (below) had three vicious-looking horns.

## HORN FACTS

● Horned dinosaurs are called ceratopsians. *Styracosaurus* had a sharp spiky collar. *Pachyrhinosaurus* had a bony knob on its nose.

*Styracosaurus*

*Pachyrhinosaurus*

# Which dinosaurs had armor?

Instead of horns, some plant eaters had thick skin which protected them like armor. These dinosaurs were called ankylosaurs. Bony spikes grew in their skin. Some even had a bony club on the end of their tail.

With one charge of its shoulder spikes, *Panoplosaurus* could seriously injure a hungry meat eater.

# What was a bonehead?

Boneheads were a group of dinosaurs with very thick skulls. They used to head-butt one another to decide who would lead the herd, like mountain goats do today. The thick skull protected the soft brain inside.

With its thick skull and stiff backbone, a bonehead was like a living battering ram.

# Which dinosaurs had back plates?

*Stegosaurus* (below) was the largest of the stegosaurs, a group of plant-eating dinosaurs with plates and spines down their backs.

**STEGOSAUR FACTS**

● The stegosaurs' plates and spines may have been used as armor, or for giving off heat from the animal's body.

*Wuerhosaurus*

*Kentrosaurus*

# Did dinosaurs lay eggs?

Like most reptiles today, young dinosaurs hatched out of eggs. Scientists have found groups of fossilized nests, some containing ten eggs or more. The eggs are small for such large animals. Smaller eggs have thinner shells, making it easier for the animal to hatch out.

*Hypsilophodon* covered its nest with a layer of sand or leaves to keep the eggs warm until they hatched.

Another way to keep eggs warm is for a parent to sit on them, as birds do today.

Some dinosaurs dug their nests in soft sand or leaves. *Protoceratops* laid its eggs in circles.

**DO YOU KNOW**

The biggest dinosaur egg ever found is only five times as big as a hen's egg.

Hen's egg

# What were baby dinosaurs like?

Newborn dinosaurs were as helpless as baby birds. They were fed by their parents until they were big enough to leave the nest.

Fossilized nests containing baby dinosaurs were found in the United States in 1978. By studying them, scientists learned a lot about the young of the dinosaur called *Maiasaura*.

**MAIASAURA FACTS**

● *Maiasaura* means "good mother lizard."

● They lived in herds, looking after their young together, and nesting at the same site each year.

The babies were fed by their parents until they could look after themselves.

Baby dinosaurs may have had a small horn on their nose to help them break out of the eggshell.

Tiny baby *Maiasaura*, as well as unhatched eggs, have been found in some of the fossilized nests.

## Could dinosaurs fly?

Dinosaurs were land animals—they couldn't fly. Another group of animals ruled the skies in dinosaur times. Called pterosaurs, they had large heads, small furry bodies, and leathery wings. They didn't have feathers. There were many kinds of pterosaur. The ones shown here all lived in Europe about 150 million years ago.

**PTEROSAUR FACTS**

● *Quetzalcoatlus* (1) was the biggest pterosaur. Its wing-span was greater than 40 feet.

● The smallest was *Batrachognathus* (2).

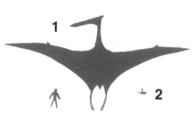

*Rhamphorhynchus* had a tail like a rudder, which helped it to steer.

**FLY A PTEROSAUR**

Draw the outline of a pterosaur on a sheet of thin cardboard. Cut it out carefully, fold it down the middle, and color it in. Weight its nose with a paperclip and watch it fly!

*Archaeopteryx* was the first bird. It was covered with feathers, but it had teeth, not a beak.

*Anurognathus* was one of the smallest pterosaurs. It had a short snout and tiny teeth. It ate insects.

Scientists can tell what a pterosaur ate by studying its jaws.

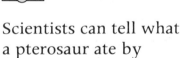

*Dzungaripterus* had a beak like pincers for crushing shellfish.

*Dimorphodon* had the strong jaws and sharp teeth of a meat eater.

*Tropeognathus* fed on fish. Its curious jaws steadied it in the water.

*Pterodactylus* had broad wings. Like many pterosaurs, it fed on fish.

# Could dinosaurs swim?

Dinosaurs couldn't swim, but there were many seagoing reptiles during the dinosaur age. The biggest belonged to a group of short- or long-necked animals with four flippers—the plesiosaurs.

Fossils of sea creatures are fairly common because their bodies naturally sank to the seabed and were buried in mud, which later turned to stone. A land animal's body had to fall into a river or lake first (see page 5).

Plesiosaurs were fast swimmers. They had four paddlelike fins which they "flapped" in the water, just as penguins do today.

*Cryptoclidus* ate fish. Its jaws were lined with sharp little teeth which were perfect for snapping up such slippery food.

At 10 feet, *Cryptoclidus* was as long as a rowboat. It could dart its long neck into schools of fish when hunting.

Plesiosaurs would sometimes attack each other. Their teethmarks have been found on fossilized bones!

### TEST OUT BODY SHAPE

Animals' bodies evolve to suit their surroundings. Sea animals' rounded bodies move through water easily.

**1** Collect together some differently shaped objects.

**2** Tie string to each one and tow it through water. Which object moves most easily?

*Stenopterygius* belonged to another group of sea reptiles called ichthyosaurs. They looked rather like today's dolphins.

### SEA REPTILE FACTS

● *Mosasaurus* was a giant sea lizard, about 34 feet long.

● *Pleurosaurus* and *Askeptosaurus* moved by lashing their tails.

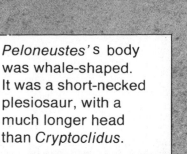

*Mosasaurus*

*Askeptosaurus*

*Pleurosaurus*

*Peloneustes*'s body was whale-shaped. It was a short-necked plesiosaur, with a much longer head than *Cryptoclidus*.

# What happened to the dinosaurs?

Suddenly they all disappeared. Dinosaurs seem to have vanished after the Cretaceous period—along with pterosaurs, sea reptiles, and many other animals. No fossils of them have ever been found in any rock younger than 65 million years old.

Scientists aren't sure what happened. Some think that giant rocks from outer space crashed into Earth sending up huge clouds of dust. Others have different ideas.

The huge dust clouds sent up by the crashing rocks would have blocked out the Sun, plunging the world into freezing darkness, and killing many of the animals very quickly.

Birds managed to survive the disaster. Maybe they were able to hide from the choking dust until it cleared.

## EXTINCTION FACTS

• Some scientists think changes in the Sun's rays weakened dinosaur eggshells and killed their young.

• Earth's continents were once closer than they are today. Dinosaurs moved from one to another and may have spread disease.

• Dinosaurs may have been poisoned by new kinds of trees and flowering plants.

Mammals survived as well. Panic-stricken, they may have burrowed underground—perhaps hibernating until life returned to normal.

The suffocating dust would have been carried on the wind for months—blocking out light and warmth from the Sun.

Dinosaurs were too big to hide. They may have frozen to death in the cold or, with the loss of all their food plants, they may have starved.

# What came after the dinosaurs?

The dinosaurs had been the ruling animals on Earth for 160 million years. When they died out, the mammals began to take over. Mammals were small, but evolved quickly. *Hyaenodon* (below) was a fierce meat eater.

**DO YOU KNOW**

Meat-eating mammals such as wolves kill their prey with long teeth near the front of their mouths. Their back teeth shear the meat—they work rather like scissors.

# Which were the biggest mammals?

A group of plant-eating mammals known as uintatheres were the giants of their day. *Uintatherium* (below) was up to 13 feet long. The group evolved 10 million years after the dinosaurs, but later died out.

**DO YOU KNOW**

Unlike meat eaters, plant eaters don't have long killing teeth. They have teeth that chop and grind their food, breaking it down before they swallow it.

# What were the first whales like?

With its small head and serpentlike body, *Basilosaurus* (below) looked very different from the whales of today. This huge sea mammal had fierce-looking teeth, and hunted fish and squid.

*Basilosaurus* still had hind feet—passed down from its land-living ancestors. Its flippers had evolved from the front legs.

# What were the first bats like?

In many ways *Icaronycteris* (below) was like modern bats—its wings were made of skin, and its sharp teeth snapped up insects as it flew. It had a long tail, however—quite different from bats today.

Unlike bats today, *Icaronycteris* had a claw on its first finger as well as its thumb. It hung from these when it roosted.

# DEATH IN THE SWAMP

*All known facts about dinosaurs and their habitats have been entered in a computer program called DINO, designed by world-famous paleontologist Dr. Karl Harlow. He has linked this up to a Virtual Reality machine, with controls that allow the operators to move through the computer-generated landscapes, as though they are living dinosaurs themselves. Dr. Harlow has devised a number of "games" that will allow him to observe how dinosaurs may have behaved under certain circumstances. To this, he has added the "Random Effect"—unpredicatable circumstances caused by the presence of the player in the game. The players are his children: Buddy, a thirteen-year-old girl, who is brilliant at computer games, and Rob, her ten-year-old brother, who is mad about dinosaurs and wants to be a paleontologist. When "playing" DINO, Buddy and Rob will have to get as close to the Virtual dinosaurs as possible. They may even have to kill to survive, or become hunted themselves, and risk "death by dinosaur!"*

*Rob felt the familiar electronic triggers inside the Virtual Reality glove, heard the static hiss in his helmet speakers as the computer booted up the DINO program, and settled himself into the VR rig in readiness for his next adventure into the computer-generated past. He was going back 150 million years at the throw of a switch—into the humid and hostile world of the Jurassic period, where huge forests flourished and huge creatures roamed in them. This was the time of the largest land-living animals that have ever walked on Earth: the gigantic sauropods. One of the tallest among them, the height of a three-story building, was Brachiosaurus. And it was this loafing, lumbering giant that Rob was about to observe.*

Rob wondered what the computer would choose for his BV or Biovehicle—the creature whose body he would "borrow" for the length of the mission. His curiosity was soon satisfied. His father spoke to him over the VR helmet speakers:

*Anurognathus*

"Your BV just came through,Rob. It's *Anurognathus*." Rob's heart sank. He had hoped for the fast-strutting *Elaphrosaurus*, or the sharp-fanged *Ceratosaurus*. But the pterosaur *Anurognathus*, about the size of a crow, looked like an overgrown puffin.

"That's just great,Dad," he said, unable to hide his disappointment.

"Take care, Rob, remember this is the first time you've flown."

The computer hummed more loudly as it switched to VR, and the screensaver of gliding pterosaurs faded. It was replaced with a thickly forested scene. Mist hung over high canopies of trees, a brown river threaded through a low flood plain, and far off was the metallic glint of a Jurassic sea. As Rob moved his finger controls, the horizon suddenly shifted, tilting the scene at a sickening angle. Rob caught his breath as he realized he was flying several hundred feet above the ground, and was clearly out of control. He tried more finger movements, and found himself upside down with the forest occupying the top half of the screen and the sky the lower half. He heard himself shriek as the screen tumbled and turned, and he crashed dizzily into the conifer trees.

He lost several vital seconds as he recovered his balance. Using his controls, he grasped a branch for all his worth. When he had stopped panting, he said, "That was terrific." He went through the orientation procedure, using his other hand on the menu buttons.

"The year counter reads 153 million years, and the clock 8:02 A.M. Locator reads East Africa, Tanzania. Weather is ... well, I can't tell because I'm in a thick mist, sitting at the top of a tree."

As he made his report, a sound like thunder vibrated in his helmet speakers. But he soon realized that this was no thunderstorm—it was a deep rumbling like bull elephants make, but twenty times louder. It was the noise, Rob then understood, made by a creature 10 times an elephant's size—a *Brachiosaurus*!

**DINODATA**

*RHAMPHORHYNCHUS*
Wingspan 3 ft.3 in.
(1 m) Long, narrow jaws
with sharp teeth
that pointed outward.
Long tail for stability.

# DINOVENTURES

The head suddenly appeared out of the mist, at the level of the conifers' upper branches. Rob tried to shrink in size, as the huge head snatched a vast quantity of leaves with its mouth only a yard from where he perched, showering the ground far below with debris. The mist was rapidly clearing as the sun rose, and he could now make out the whole shape of the enormous creature. The tail, all 23 feet (7 m) of it, and as long as a derrick crane neck, scythed at the rear. Rob wondered if these were just counterbalancing movements, or a type of rearguard defense to

Rob landed clumsily upon the back of the brachiosaur.

ALERT

Year
153 MY

V. Time
08.02

EXIT

RANDOM
EFFECT

ENERGY

prevent surprise attacks. Rob remembered reading somewhere that these animals may have had two brains—one in their heads, and another secondary nerve center near the tails. Perhaps the rear legs and tail were under the control of the secondary brain.

The first adult that had fed on this treetop refuge was followed by three more adults and two juveniles. Rob assumed they were making the low frequency rumbling noise to communicate with the main herd, a bit like whales do across vast ocean distances. Gently steaming, like a flotilla of ocean liners through a sea of foliage, these landbound giants left a wake of devastation as they passed onward.

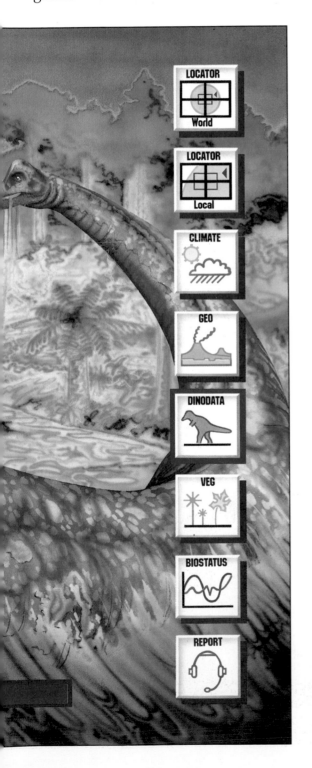

LOCATOR
World

LOCATOR
Local

CLIMATE

GEO

DINODATA

VEG

BIOSTATUS

REPORT

He knew he could not stay perched in the tree while the DINO program ran through its precious minutes. He had to make a move—and either fly safely, or fall to the ground and out, most likely, of DINO. He launched himself into the air with gentle movements of his finger controls. The screen somersaulted again, but less violently than before. He brought the horizon under control, and found to his amazement that he was gaining height as he was lifted by a thermal current of rising air. He rose above the conifers, and gained a superb view of the East African scene once more. Way below he saw the gently plodding family of brachiosaurs moving toward a group of ten or so others over to the west. It was toward these that he now began to fly.

As he moved the controls, he tumbled in the air. A whooshing noise, the flap of leathery wings, and a loud scream was all he knew about the attack from *Rhamphorhynchus*, a predatory pterosaur. It banked in the air for another attempt, its jaw opening to reveal teeth like broken bottles. Rob dived for the cover of trees, some hundred feet below. The Rhampo followed—with its slightly greater bulk and bigger wingspan it began to gain on Rob. He tucked his wings behind him, and fell like an arrow, only leveling out when under the tree canopy. The Rhampo continued to chase through the trees, but Rob was beginning to master his flight controls at last, and threw a quick combination of maneuvers. This was Virtual Reality at its most exciting, and Rob thrilled at every moment. He heard the sound of crashing undergrowth and splintering branches and saw ahead the herd of brachiosaurs. He also noticed for the first time the *Anurognathuses*—identical to his BV—sitting on their backs. As he flew toward

**LOCATOR**
**World**

them, the teeth of his enemy closed on his wing tip. At the same time, a cluster of *Anurognathus* rose from the backs of the brachiosaurs and flew straight at him. There was a fearful scream from the *Rhamphorhynchus* as the thirty or more smaller, puffinlike pterosaurs tore at it with their razor-sharp beaks.

**VEG**

Rob landed clumsily upon the back of a brachiosaur and gripped its ridged flesh with his needlelike talons. Rob clicked on his energy level and saw it had dropped to 3.5. He needed rest or food. Or both.

**REPORT**

The flock of Anuros flew back with much cawing and croaking. They settled on the rising and falling backs of the Brachios, and scurried over the vast surfaces of rutted skin, pecking with their stubby beaks as they did so. Rob saw to his horror what they were doing, and what he himself would have to do. There were white and bloated ticks the size of small potatoes hanging to the Brachio's skin, hideously long centipedes snaking through the folds of flesh, and bloodsucking flies gorging themselves on the crops of worm-infested wounds around the Brachio's neck. On this repulsive picnic the Anuros were greedily feasting. Rob steeled himself, and did likewise, until his energy level rose a little. Soothed by the sound of the deep rumbling song of his host dinosaur, he closed his eyes and rested.

In real time only a few minutes had passed, but in Virtual Time it had been hours. When he opened his eyes, the forest was in moonlight. He was still on the back of the Brachio, but he had to cling on as the huge animal lurched and rolled. It was plain the Brachio was in trouble. It bellowed and snorted, and lashed its tail. Each time the tail fell, a wall of foul water rose into the air. A chorus of squawks rose into the dark canopy of ancient trees and, as Rob looked over the vast bulk of the Brachio's rump, he saw a marauding pack of *Elaphrosaurus* terrifying the beast. They darted in and nipped its treelike legs with their ferociously sharp teeth. Before the Brachio could react, they had sped away to

A herd of *Brachiosaurus*

a safe distance.  Rob understood at once that the *Elaphrosaurus* pack was driving the brachiosaur—either deliberately or by chance—into a swamp.  Its many tons of flesh were forcing its huge legs further into the swamp. It was sinking under its own weight, and its death was inescapable. Rob could see the other brachiosaurs standing farther off, rumbling and trumpeting in obvious distress.  One of their species was about to meet a slow and untimely end.

Even as Rob flew off the back of the rapidly exhausting brachiosaur,  he recognized the menacing shape of a late Jurassic crocodile slide into the waters. In the ghostly electronic moonlight, Rob shuddered with disgust as he heard the brachiosaur roar and hiss with pain, as the crocodile found its mark. Its hunger would soon be satisfied.

The elaphrosaurs, too, had become more daring. They squawked like oversized chickens, and drove the brachiosaur nearer to its doom. Now sunk beyond its knees, it lacked the strength to pull itself from the swamp. Its struggles only forced it farther into the ooze.

Very close to the time limit in DINO, Rob exited with feelings of great sadness for the stricken and helpless beast. As he unhooked the VR harness, he exchanged looks with his sister. Buddy had been following his progress on the monitor, and had seen the sad end of the brachiosaur. She put her arm around Rob as Dr. Harlow quietly explained:

"What you may have witnessed there, Rob, was a species no longer in harmony with its environment. The brachiosaurs needed vast quantities of fuel, and to find it they had to stay constantly on the move. When food got scarce, they had to move to hostile country —like swamps. It was a choice between death by starvation, or death by . . . well, you saw what happened."

"But it was so cruel. It didn't stand a chance," Rob said.

"Animals in the wild are not known for their kindness to each other—even now," Dr. Harlow said, as he closed down the computer.

To cheer him up, Buddy said: "At least you know how to fly by VR now. You were great flying through those trees."

Rob smiled, pleased by the compliment.

"I'm starving," he said, and realized he really was ravenous.

"That's good," Buddy said, "because we're having your favorite supper—boiled ticks and fried centipedes."

# ESCAPE FROM T. REX

The computer had selected Buddy to enter DINO for the one role she dreaded most—to observe and possibly confront Tyrannosaurus rex. As with all impressionable children, Buddy had held T. rex in total awe since she was very small. She remembered the toys both she and Rob had enjoyed as kids. These were hard rubber monsters, crudely painted with blood-splashed jaws, plastic transformers with batteries that powered flashing red eyes, and a soft cuddly T. rex with button eyes and a stupid grin. She remembered the toys lined along bookshelves in her bedroom, and felt again the terror when her father switched off the light, and the shadows of her toys, cast by the filtered street lights, reared up and lengthened against the bedroom wall. She had stayed awake some nights, until sheer exhaustion had eased her into sleep.

The VR glove

"If you would prefer not to do this, Buddy, I don't mind if you give *T. rex* a miss. Even in a computer program he is probably best avoided," Karl Harlow had said, as she pulled on the Virtual Reality helmet.

"No Dad. I'm going to meet it face to face," she said, sounding braver than she really felt. It would be like seeing a horror movie, she told herself. *T. rex* could do her no more harm than a TV bug-eyed monster. But she knew that Virtual Reality was very different from sitting in an armchair, watching TV in the same room as your family. Very different.

She finished adjusting the VR equipment and said into the small mike: "OK Dad. Ready to meet Mr. Nasty."

"Just getting your BV through. Looks as though you're in luck. It's a Quetz." This was their name for *Quetzalcoatlus*—the gigantic flying pterosaur. In the computer program she would have all its physical abilities. The screensaver of circling *Pteranodon*s faded, and gave way to a breathtaking view . . . far below her was an anicent sea, its waves breaking on a late Cretaceous shore. A broad, flat river delta spilled from a vast flood plain. In the misty distance were mountains, and wisps of smoke suggesting volcanic activity.

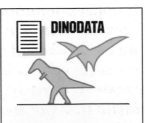

*Edmontosaurus with its young*

Buddy—as a *Quetzalcoatlus*—tried her flight controls by moving her fingers in the VR glove. "This is beautiful," she said, as the huge wings of the Quetz dipped, and made her begin a graceful spiraling descent toward the delta and the horrors it held. She began her report: "Somewhere near modern Seattle, visibility good, temperature is 105 degrees Fahrenheit, humidity high. Vegetation is quite a mix: ferns, palms, figs, and sycamores, with groves of magnolias. Selecting DINODATA. Family of *Triceratops* browsing the magnolias directly below me, a herd of *Edmontosaurus* way off to the south, two *Pachycephalosaurus* approaching this area, an *Ankylosaurus* a mile east, and there he is—old Mr. Nasty, an adult *Tyrannosaurus*, one click north of here and approaching. I suddenly feel a bit sick."

Buddy glided over the shimmering waters of the delta, moving the large counterbalanced head of her Quetz Biovehicle in search of her quarry. She saw the *Triceratops* first. It swiveled its head

**DINODATA**

*TRICERATOPS*
27 feet long.
Bulky body.
Massive head, with
deep parrotlike
beak and neck frill
with bony bumps.

upward as her shadow passed over, and revealed its armored neck frill, edged with a zigzag of bony knobs. Its two massive horns looked terrifyingly sharp. It was quietly and calmly cropping the huge magnolia blooms with its oversized beak of a mouth. "I've found a *Triceratops*," Buddy said into her headset, "Mr. T is probably not far from here. I'm going to take a look." With a few downbeats of those enormous leathery wings, Buddy lifted herself high above the flood plain. Without warning, a *Tyrannosaurus* burst through the magnolias in several enormous

"*T. rex* bounded after her and made a lunge with its teeth-laden head."

ALERT

Year
70 MY

V. Time
06.28

EXIT

RANDOM
EFFECT

ENERGY

strides that shook the ground. Still gliding some 500 feet above this scene, Buddy wheeled in a large circle to see what the *Tyrannosaurus* would do now. It was her mission, after all, to observe and if possible *interact* with the dinosaurs in her program.

From the safety of her airborne observatory, this most feared of all carnosaurs did not seem so terrifying. Its puny arms looked like pipe cleaners, stuck on its body as an afterthought. But as Buddy's shadow passed over it, the *Tyrannosaurus* looked up and opened its vast jaw the width of a child's outstretched arms. This mighty jaw was fringed with teeth like hunting knives, some missing, some broken—all daggers. It uttered its terrible roar of hunger and snapped its jaws together. Buddy shuddered.

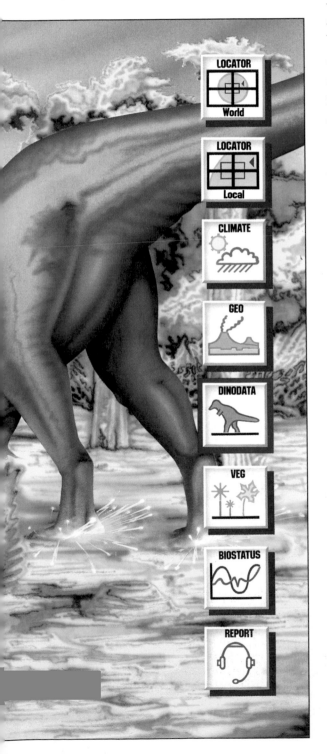

She then realized that the *Triceratops* was still on her screen. Unable to retreat, as there was a wall of rock behind it, the Tric had remained watchful and quiet—its fearsome horns following the *Tyrannosaurus*, wherever it moved. And *T. rex* was now sniffing the air. It knew that meat was nearby, but the Tric was partly concealed by magnolia trees. As Buddy's shadow passed over the Tric, it turned its head upward. The *Tyrannosaurus* caught the movement and swung its rectangular block of a head toward the Tric. With a roar of triumph, *T. rex* bounded with surprising speed through the magnolias and confronted the cornered herbivore. There was a moment of stillness as the two dinosaurs weighed each other up, then, with a roar the *Tyrannosaurus* lunged at the Tric. Buddy saw a flash of teeth, and *T. rex* had the Tric by the neck frill. The Tric violently shook its head and a horn stabbed *T. rex* just below one of its flailing arms. With a bellow of pain and surprise, the *Tyrannosaurus* lifted its great head, and then dropped it like a hammer on the exposed neck of the Tric. It was over quickly. Buddy heard the sound of crunching vertebrae as *T. rex*'s teeth found their mark. The Tric leaned sideways, sunk to its knees, and then fell heavily into the dust. Buddy watched in horror as the *Tyrannosaurus* began to feed on the still dying beast.

Still gliding above this horrific happening on the ground below, Buddy saw a puff of dust followed a second or so later by a loud *crumpf*. Two *Pachycephalosaurus* were performing their ancient ritual of head-to-head duels. They stood about 50 feet apart and pawed the ground, raising dust.

At some unseen signal, each animal rushed at great speed on two birdlike legs toward its oncoming target. The bony heads met with a sharp crack and one animal, clearly stunned, made a wobbly retreat, while the other prepared itself for another attack.

The second charge was interrupted by a thunderous bellow from the *Tyrannosaurus*, who objected to being distracted from its grisly meal. Both of the head bangers, their battle forgotten, crashed through the magnolia grove, and away from Buddy's field of vision.

She was lifted high above the flood plain on a sudden updraught of warm air and felt a wonderful wave of relief at being distanced from *T. rex*'s jaws. Below she spotted the herd of *Edmontosaurus*, disturbed by some unseen predator, stampeding northward across the plain. She mentally willed them not to come too close to the *Tyrannosaurus*. She saw, too, the pair of rival *Pachycephalosaurus*, sizing each other up near a clump of dogwoods. Buddy's observations were interrupted by a flashing warning light—it told her that her energy level was critical. She needed food urgently. Meat, preferably carrion. With a sickening realization she knew exactly where to find it.

*Alphadon* (left) with *Gypsonictops*

There was but one thing to do. She had to return to the Tric and feed on what remained of it. She just hoped that the *Tyrannosaurus* had moved on. As she glided down to the rocks where the Tric had been savagely killed, Buddy moved her VR helmet from side to side, searching for signs of the *T. rex*. It was nowhere to be seen. She could make out the badly butchered corpse of the Tric. Its rib cage stuck in the air like a huge shopping basket. Buddy floated down and with expert use of her finger controls brought the Quetz to a halt a few feet from the Tric. It was then she understood why the *Quetzalcoatlus* spent so much time in the air—on the ground it was a clumsy contraption. Its enormous wings dragged along behind her, as she tried to hop and crawl the few feet to her energy source.

Buddy closed her mind to what she was doing and fed. She was pleased to see her energy levels rise with each disgusting beakful of *Triceratops* flesh. But her relief was short-lived when she heard the blood-chilling roar of the *Tyrannosaurus*. She felt the ground vibrate with each of its terrible footfalls. It had come to claim its unfinished meal, and Buddy was caught in the act of stealing it. She had to get airborne as quickly as possible. That was her only escape. She hopped off the Tric carcass and loped away from the approaching *Tyrannosaurus*. It bounded after her and made a lunge with its teeth-laden head. It missed, but only by inches. Buddy, even in her terror, knew that *T. rex* was slower than when it had attacked the Tric. As she struggled to open her wings, she remembered to hit the Random Effect control. It might suddenly give the *Tyrannosaurus* extra strength, cause a flood, make a volcano, drop a meteorite—she had no idea. But when she hit the screen menu, the wind strengthened, straightened out her wings, and lifted her off the ground. *T. rex* made a desperate biting jump as she was lifted above it. The teeth snapped together on empty space. She swiveled her electronic head down to see the dying *Tyrannosaurus* slumped on its side, the wound made by the *Triceratops*'s horns now bleeding freely. Numerous *Alphadon*, small omniverous marsupials, were already gathering under nearby trees, to feed upon the greatest meat eater of them all.

"The second charge was interrupted by a thunderous bellow from the *Tyrannosaurus*."

Another warning signal told Buddy she would have to exit from DINO, or lose precious points. She looked down upon the gasping *Tyrannosaurus* with mixed feelings of horror and sadness, her childhood fears finally laid to rest. With her *Quetzalcoatlus*'s claw, she pressed EXIT. The screensaver image returned to tell her she was now out of DINO. Pulling off the VR helmet, she was relieved to see the familiar faces of her brother Rob, and her father, Dr. Harlow. They greeted her as though she had been away for over 70 million years. Which, in a way, she had.

# Glossary

**Ankylosaur** ("stiff reptile") An armored dinosaur with bony plates and a club at the end of its tail. A group that existed in the Jurassic and Cretaceous periods.

**badlands** Open lands, particularly in North America, where there are very few plants. The land surface erodes rapidly because rainfall can wash away soil and surface rock. Normally, plants stop this. Badlands may contain deep valleys and high rock pinnacles.

**bipedal** ("two-footed") Walking on two legs.

**Brachiosaurids** ("arm reptiles") Giant-sized, four-legged, plant-eating dinosaurs with long necks, deep bodies, heavy legs, and a short, thick tail; includes *Brachiosaurus* and its cousins.

**browser** An animal that feeds on the shoots of bushes and trees.

**butte** A tall, straight-sided mass of rock in a badlands area that has been eroded all around by wind and rain. The butte may have escaped erosion because it has a cap of hard rock that was not worn away.

**carnivore** ("meat eater") An animal that eats other animals.

**Carnosaur** ("meat reptile") A large carnivorous dinosaur.

**community** Plants and animals living together in one area; the animals either feed upon the plants (herbivores), or each other (carnivores).

**conifer** A type of evergreen tree, usually with cones and needlelike leaves.

**continent** A major land mass such as Africa, Europe, or North America.

**coral reef** A small island or reef formed by coral—a small marine invertebrate, usually living in a colony.

**Cretaceous** ("of the chalk") The third and final period of the "Age of Dinosaurs"—from 145 to 65 million years ago.

**cycad** A tropical, or subtropical, palmlike plant.

**cycadeoid** An extinct plant, resembling a cycad, but only distantly related.

**Deinonychosaur** ("fearful claw reptile") A meat-eating dinosaur, belonging to a group of active hunters that are best known in the Cretaceous. Typical members include *Deinonychus* and *Velociraptor*.

**dinosaur** ("terrible reptile") One of a group of advanced reptiles common in the Mesozoic era.

**Diplocids** ("double beams") A family of very large and long, four-legged, plant-eating dinosaurs; includes *Dryosaurus*.

**Dromaeosaur** ("running reptile") A birdlike theropod dinosaur with a stiff tail and large toe claws.

**Dryosaurids** ("oak reptiles") Small to medium-sized, two-legged, plant-eating dinosaurs; includes *Dryosaurus*.

**endocast** ("internal cast") A fossil replica of the inside of the braincase (endocranial case).

**erosion** The wearing away of rocks and soil by wind, rain, rivers, and the sea.

**evolution** ("unrolling") The way in which plants and animals have changed through time.

**extinction** ("disappearing") The dying out of a group of plants or animals.

**fauna** The animals of a particular region or period.

**food chain** The normal passage of food through living communities. The chain begins with plants, which are eaten by plant-eating animals. The plant eaters are then eaten by meat eaters, and these in turn may be eaten by bigger meat eaters. In the end, the dead bodies of animals break down and are eaten by microbes. They then form food for the plants.

**formation** In geology, a large named unit of rock with some common characteristics.

**gastroliths** Stones that helped a dinosaur's digestive processes by lodging in its gizzard, where they ground plant food into a pulp.

**ginkgo** A primitive tree with fan-shaped leaves, probably eaten by dinosaurs.

**gizzard** A muscular portion of the stomach, where the food is ground up, often with the help of gastroliths (stomach stones).

**Hadrosaur** ("big reptile") A duckbilled ornithopod dinosaur.

**herbivore** ("plant eater") An animal that eats only plants.

**intestine** A long muscular tube, part of the digestive system, in which food is broken down and absorbed into the body.

**Jurassic** ("Jura-age," after the Jura Mountains of France, which are made of rocks from this time) The second or middle period of the "Age of Dinosaurs"—from 205 to 145 million years ago.

**Lambeosaur** ("Lambe reptile," after the Canadian paleontologist Lawrence Lambe) A duckbilled dinosaur with a bony crest on its head.

**mammal** ("suckling animal") A warm-blooded, backboned animal, covered in hair, and feeding its young with milk; mice, bats, cats, dolphins, horses, and humans are all mammals.

**marsupial** A mammal that rears its young in a pouch on its belly.

**mass extinction** The dying out of many different kinds of plants or animals at the same time.

**Mesozoic** ("middle life") The whole of the "Age of Dinosaurs," consisting of the Triassic, Jurassic, and Cretaceous periods. It lasted from 245 to 65 million years ago.

**monsoon** A rainy season controlled by changing winds.

**muscle** A strong, fibrous fleshy part of the body, that runs from one bone to another, and moves that part of the body.

**nocturnal** Animals that feed and move around at night.

**organism** A living creature, including animals, plants, fungi, and microbes.

**Ornithomimid** ("bird mimic") A toothless theropod dinosaur of the dinosaur family Ornithomimidae.

**Ornithopod** ("bird foot") Small to medium-sized, plant-eating dinosaur that could stand on two legs and had a stiff tail; includes *Dryosaurus* and the duckbills.

**Pachycephalosaur** ("thick-headed reptile") A dome-headed, two-legged, plant-eating dinosaur.

**paleontologist** ("ancient life studier") A scientist who studies prehistoric life and its fossil evidence.

**predator** A meat-eating animal that hunts and kills other animals for food.

**protein** The basic chemical units that make up plants and animals.

**Pterosaur** ("wing reptile") Ancient flying reptile with wings of skin rather than feathers. Not a dinosaur.

**reptile** ("creeping one") A scaled, cold-blooded, backboned animal, such as a turtle, lizard, snake, crocodile, or dinosaur.

**Sauropod** ("reptile foot") Large, four-legged plant eater with a long neck and long tail. Member of a group of dinosaurs that lived in Jurassic and Cretaceous times.

**scavenger** An animal that feeds on either dead or dying animals.

**sediment** Small bits of rock in the form of gravel, sand, and mud.

**seed fern** A tropical or subtropical fernlike plant bearing seeds.

**species** A group of living things that are similar to each other and can inter-breed. The basic unit of classification.

**spinal plexus** A swelling of the spinal cord at the spot near the hip where many lesser nerves meet.

**Stegosaur** ("roofed reptile") A plant-eating dinosaur with a combination of bony plates and spines along its back and tail.

**subtropical** Areas of the world that lie just north and south of the tropics.

**Theropod** ("beast foot") A two-legged, meat-eating dinosaur. Includes tyrannosaurs and birds.

**Thyreophora** ("shield bearers") The dinosaur group that includes the stegosaurs and ankylosaurs.

**Titanosaurids** ("titantic reptiles") Small to large-sized sauropods that lived from the late Jurassic to the late Cretaceous. They include *Saltasaurus* and *Titanosaurus*.

**toxin** A natural poison produced by an organism.

**trackway** A line of footprints left by an animal walking across soft ground.

**Triassic** ("three-part") The first part of the "Age of Dinosaurs"—from 245 to 205 million years ago.

**Troodontid** ("wounding tooth") A small theropod dinosaur with large eyes and a relatively small brain.

**tropical** Areas of the world that lie around the equator.

**Tyrannosaur** ("tyrant reptile") A large carnivorous dinosaur from the latter part of the Cretaceous period. Includes *Tyrannosaurus* and its cousins.

# Index